THE
PRACTICING
WRITER

THE PRACTICING WRITER

Arthur H. Bell
California State University, Fullerton

Thomas P. Klammer
California State University, Fullerton

Houghton Mifflin Company   Boston
Dallas   Geneva, Illinois   Hopewell, New Jersey
Palo Alto   London

Cover illustration by Ken Maryanski.

Printed in the U.S.A.

Library of Congress Catalog Card Number: 82-83411

ISBN: 0-395-32564-1

Contents

Preface

Reading about writing is like reading about running: you still have to run to run well and write to write well. We wrote *The Practicing Writer* for students who want to write—and write well. In each chapter, concise instruction, clear examples, and numerous exercises provide a series of writing experiences designed to build students' abilities and confidence in the fundamental skills of writing. Throughout the text, our purpose is to prepare beginning writers for the writing they will do in their college courses, and we have organized the text so that students can practice their way toward good writing skills.

Step by step, *The Practicing Writer* teaches effective writing of paragraphs and short essays along with the basics of style, grammar, and mechanics. Part One, "A Guide to Writing," begins with several experiments designed to overcome "audience worry" and to underscore the importance of purpose in writing. Chapters 2, 3, and 4 discuss and provide practice in three paragraph forms useful for college writing: the assertive paragraph, the descriptive paragraph, and the narrative paragraph. In Chapter 5, students continue to practice paragraph forms while mastering fifteen practical matters of style. In Chapter 6, students turn to the essay and practice several invention techniques and methods of organization designed to overcome the dread of longer, more complex writing assignments.

Throughout Part One, sample paragraphs illustrate the principles of effective writing and serve as models for students' own writing. These principles are reinforced through a series of carefully paced exercises that ask students to revise sentences and paragraphs or to write their own. Each chapter includes a recap of the major points discussed in the text and ends with suggested writing assignments that specify a situation, audience, and purpose for each topic.

In Part Two, students develop their ability to produce carefully edited final drafts through diagnosis, practice, and mastery of basic grammar and mechanics skills. Each skill is practiced in a series of exercises that supplement the instructional portion of each chapter. First, the text introduces some basic vocabulary for talking about parts of sentences and then turns to a range of sentence problems, from sentence fragments and agreement to matters of conventional punctuation and capitalization. Instructors may choose to intersperse grammar and mechanics chapters among the writing lessons assigned from Part One, to selectively assign chapters in grammar and mechanics as individual or class needs become apparent from the diagnostic tests found throughout Part Two, or to teach Part Two consecutively from beginning to end.

Following Part Two, there are three short appendices: guidelines on spelling, stages in a sample essay (as discussed in Chapter 6), and a brief introduction to writing the research paper.

We wish to thank the following individuals who read the manuscript of *The Practicing Writer* and made many helpful suggestions: Susan Carey, Community College of Philadelphia; Sandra Edinger, Kirkhof College, Allendale, Michigan; Ann Matsuhashi, University of Illinois at Chicago Circle; Louis B. Queary, Central Oregon Community College; and David E. Schwalm, The University of Texas at El Paso.

Writing this text has brought us satisfaction. We lay down our pens with anticipation, knowing that practicing writers will pick them up.

A. H. B.
T. P. K.

THE
PRACTICING
WRITER

PART ONE

A Guide to Writing

Writing—like singing, dancing, and dreaming—makes us happy to be human. But like other great and fine things, writing can frighten us. We set our pens to paper, pouring *ourselves* out along with the ink for all to see and judge. That's frightening. At times, we try to write and nothing pours out—no sense, no self, no satisfaction. That's frustrating.

Part One, "A Guide to Writing," deals with fright and frustration the way a dancing instructor deals with a wallflower. "Come on," the instructor says, "I'll show you a few basic steps." The paragraph, of course, is the writer's basic step. In Part One, you'll learn to write several kinds of paragraphs. You're dancing! While you're out on the floor, you can practice a few tips on movement and grace (fifteen matters of style in Chapter 5). Then, in Chapter 6, you can put your whole act together in a major performance, the essay.

Dancing instructors and English professors know that their students won't always—shouldn't always—dance or write strictly by the numbers. We want you to understand that our suggested patterns for writing in Part One are intended as helpful first steps, not rigid rules. "A Guide to Writing" gets you moving in certain steps and patterns so that, in time, you can take the lead, discovering and developing patterns of your own.

Chapter 1

Preparing to Write

Let's begin our work together with an experiment instead of a sermon.

Experiment | We call this experiment the jotting game. Jot down a single word that comes to mind for each of the words below.

Example: balloon   pop

1. chocolate   _____

2. mosquito   _____

3. corner   _____

4. dizzy   _____

5. beach   _____

6. tattered   _____

7. July   _____

8. ice   _____

Now, please evaluate this exercise by checking one box.

I found this exercise ⬰ easy ⬰ difficult.

You may be interested to know that in our sampling, most college writers found the jotting game quite easy ("about as difficult as breathing," one said). If you, too, found the experiment easy, consider an important question: *why* is writing—in this case jotting down words—sometimes so effortless and natural?

In the jotting experiment, you didn't have much to worry about. You didn't worry, for example, that you would be graded on your choice of words. You didn't worry about impressing others. You didn't even have to worry about making good sense: chocolate *islands* are just as acceptable as chocolate *cookies*. In a whimsical, relaxed way, you simply let words flow onto the page as they came into your mind.

You probably don't need to be reminded that writing is seldom so easy. Writing, in fact, is an agonizing experience for many students. A short term paper can mean dozens of false starts, countless wads of typing paper thrown in the trash, and even the humiliation of buying someone else's slap-dash work at an outrageous price.

What force interrupts that free, easy flow of words experienced in the jotting game? For many writers, the culprit is *audience worry*. They feel threatened by cold, judgmental readers. In the next experiment, consider for yourself the effects of audience worry.

Experiment

Choose an older relative, perhaps a grandparent. Answer the following question as if you were writing a letter to this relative: How would I spend $500 won on a TV gameshow?

_____

_____

_____

_____

_____

_____

_____

Evaluate your experience.

I found this experiment ⧄ more ⧄ less difficult than the jotting game.

Did you feel the weight of a new worry—the *audience worry*—in your effort to write? Let's say, for example, that you chose to write to your Uncle Wilmar, a pharmacist in Kansas City. You may have wanted to spend the $500 on a stereo system, but you envisioned Uncle Wilmar shaking his con-servative head in disapproval. So you considered spending half of the $500 on the stereo and saving the other half. Uncle Wilmar would now be pleased, but *you* feel hollow because you don't really want to save any of the money. Here's the point: the more we consider what others will think about us, the more difficult writing becomes. (Notice, by the way, how easy the letter to Uncle Wilmar would be if you simply wrote to tell him that you put the $500 into savings for pharmacy school. We relax when our audience approves of our thoughts and actions, and language flows more freely.)

1a Controlling Audience Worry

Except when you write in a diary or private journal, you tailor your words to the tastes, desires, and abilities of other people. You avoid words your readers won't understand. You build upon their set of interests. In short, you try to marry what *you* want to say with what *they* want to hear.

This writing task is less difficult when your audience loves, or at least likes you. A letter to your best friend, for example, may flow easily from your pen—the writing is *fun,* because you're not worried about your friend's judgment or reaction. What you want to say fits hand-in-glove with what your friend wants to hear. You relax and the words flow.

But often you must write to audiences that do not feel warm and accepting toward you. Then, too often, writing grinds to a halt, and the tip of the pen sits motionless on the blank paper, waiting, waiting. In our third experiment, try to locate the kind of audience that might thwart the free flow of your writing.

Experiment

Imagine that you have to write a short essay titled, "My Goals." Write *best* by the audience that would make you most comfortable; write *worst* by the audience that would make the writing most difficult.

_____ Your essay will be read by college professors you don't know.

_____ Your essay will be read by executives at a company where you are applying for a job.

_____ Your essay will be read by the minister, priest, or rabbi at your church.

_____ Your essay will be read by a congressional representative with whom you are not acquainted.

_____ Your essay will be read by six of your old high school teachers.

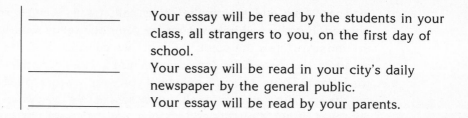

_____ Your essay will be read by the students in your class, all strangers to you, on the first day of school.

_____ Your essay will be read in your city's daily newspaper by the general public.

_____ Your essay will be read by your parents.

Take a moment to think through the specific worries that come to mind when you think of the audience you selected as "worst." Try to picture, for example, the faces of your hostile readers as they look at your essay. Are they laughing? Are they sneering in disgust? Are they simply bored? Are they disappointed in you? Are they shocked? No wonder we have so much trouble writing for these audiences! It is excruciatingly difficult to write when each word we set down brings frowns or sneers to the faces in our imagined audience.

By contrast—for relief—picture the faces in your "best" audience. Notice how interested and understanding they seem to be. They like what they read and want more. We discover that we have a great deal to say to such people. We write and write, and we do it with a sense of caring.

Unfortunately, we are not always free to write only for our "best" audiences. Important essays will be handed over to strangers—professors, classmates, employers, and the general public. We can't count on their interest, much less their kindness or respect. How, then, can we avoid the paralysis of our writing powers that such "worst" audiences always seem to bring?

First, consciously *change the faces* in your audience. Imagine that you are writing to people who sincerely want to hear what you have to say, who are willing to be patient and understanding, who wish you well. Out of a group of seemingly gruff executives, choose or invent one who cares about the things you care about. Consciously write your essay to her. Out of a group of college professors ready to pounce on any error, choose or invent a friendly face—perhaps a teacher who reminds you of a friend. Write your essay for him.

Through such mind-games, you can *control* your audience, instead of *being controlled.* Your brief fantasy makes a "worst" audience into a "best" audience and breaks the paralysis brought on by wondering "What will they think?"

Along the way, you pay your audience an important compliment. You assume that you are writing to reasonable, sensitive human beings. Your tone communicates warmth and respect toward them. Wonderfully, in language as in life, we create the reality we wish for. "Worst" audiences become "best" audiences (or at least "bearable" audiences) when we learn to think the "best" of *them*.

Experiment   In the space provided, write down the audience you selected in the previous experiment as your "worst" audience. Jot down the features of two "worst" faces from that audience; then conjure up two "best" faces from the same audience. An example is shown.

My "Worst" audience: _____
                          (Fill-in from previous experiment)

Worst Face   Best Face
nervous eyes, heavy brows,   *sparkling eyes, pleasant smile*
deep frown

Worst Face No. 1   Best Face No. 1

_____   _____

_____   _____

_____   _____

Worst Face No. 2   Best Face No. 2

_____   _____

_____   _____

_____   _____

After you have changed the faces in your audience, learn to *grasp your purpose*. Writing to a strange and judgmental audience is like being on stage for the first time. The experience is unbearably painful if we have nothing to do but stand there, hands in pockets, awkwardly shifting from foot to foot. But if we have a little routine—a tap dance, a bit of magic, a joke or two—we can forget about the staring eyes and concentrate instead on our purpose for being on stage. The more we concentrate on our little act, the more we relax. Often, we end up winning the applause of the audience we feared.

1b   Grasping Your Purpose

Writing always has a purpose, a reason for being on stage. Writers who grasp their sense of purpose seldom feel ill at ease before their audiences. They have something of importance to communicate. They have a reason for taking up someone else's time. They have a purpose.

Your purpose is simply what you want your words *to do.* In writing about government loans to students, for example, you may have an *assertive* purpose: to argue against budget cuts in student aid. In writing about a ferocious lightning storm, you may have a *descriptive* purpose: to share what you saw and heard. In writing about a man struck by lightning, you may have a *narrative* purpose: to tell others what happened.

A writer must first grasp a sense of purpose. Practice deciding on a purpose for each of the essay topics in the following experiment.

Experiment

For each of the following topics, decide on a purpose—a goal, a target—to pursue in writing to the general public. You may want to describe the topic. You may want to assert an opinion. You may want to narrate a story about the topic. Some examples are provided.

Topic	*Statement of Purpose*
Shadows	I would describe the shadows that frightened me years ago at summer camp.
Water Sports	I would assert that water polo requires extraordinary stamina.
Heroism	I would narrate the story of the first American Indians taken back to England.
1. Furniture	
2. Desserts	
3. Diets	

4. Crime _____

      _____

5. Books _____

      _____

6. Tahiti _____

      _____

The rest of this text is devoted to one goal: helping you achieve your purpose in words, sentences, paragraphs, and essays. In working toward this goal, you will experience moments when all the words went that-a-way, moments of paralysis and frustration. We hope that you will return often to the two self-rescue techniques described in this chapter:

1. Put a "best" face on a threatening audience.
2. Grasp your purpose firmly; it will always give you something to talk about when the audience seems to be staring at you mercilessly.

More often, we hope, you will experience moments that surprise you—moments when the task of writing becomes a pleasure, not a chore. Such well-wishing may seem farfetched right now, especially for those students who have experienced the "agony of defeat" more often than the "thrill of victory" in English classes. But give writing a chance. *The Practicing Writer* is designed to offer a progressive series of success experiences in writing. Page by page, you may begin to feel good about yourself as a writer, good about your audience, and good about your purpose. Don't fight the feeling.

Chapter 2

Writing Assertive Paragraphs

All paragraphs have common characteristics. Consider shape, for example. Which of the following shapes best represents a traditional paragraph?

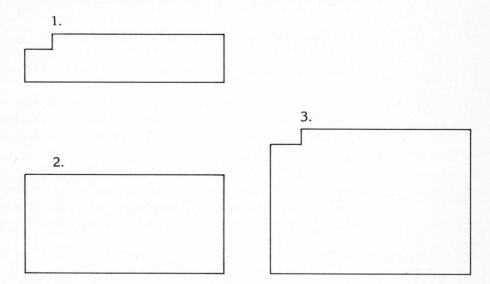

1.

2.

3.

In correctly choosing the third shape, you observed two important characteristics of the paragraph:

1. The first line is *indented* (five spaces when typing, about an inch when writing).
2. *Several* sentences usually go together to make up a paragraph. One sentence paragraphs do exist, of course, and can be useful to the writer. We'll deal with them later.

Now look at an actual paragraph. Inner divisions have been numbered. Notice that each division has a function in creating the meaning of the paragraph. Using the corresponding blanks below, decide for yourself the function for each of the inner divisions of the paragraph. Then compare your ideas with the conclusions just below the blanks.

[1] Success in some activities depends as much on relaxation as on concentration. [2] Undue tension, even when well intentioned, often blocks the free flow of both muscular and mental effort. [3] Professional golfers know that "trying too hard" can send drives slicing and putts squirting. Writers, too, face blocks born of effort and exasperation. At times the words just won't come. Relief is close at hand, of course: a moment's pause, a deep breath, perhaps a trip to the refrigerator. [4] The block is broken by trying not to try.

Briefly describe the purpose of each numbered part.

1. _____

2. _____

3. _____

4. _____

Compare your ideas with these suggestions:

1. States the topic or main idea
2. Expands the main idea
3. Illustrates (provides examples) for the main idea
4. Concludes by answering the question, "So what? So what if the rest of the paragraph is true?"

Paragraphs may be thought of as boxes containing information. Their size and internal construction depend on what you, the writer, wish to "carry" effectively to your reader.

Glance through a book, magazine, or newspaper (preferably all three). Notice the incredible variety of paragraph "boxes." Some stretch a page or more in length; others are only a few words long. But long or short, all paragraphs have one central purpose. Decide what that purpose is, then state it in the space provided.

_____

_____

_____

Compare your conclusion with this assertion: *paragraphs group related ideas together and keep them separate from other groups of related ideas.*

In this chapter and in Chapters 3 and 4, you will learn how to write the three types of paragraphs most useful for college and career writing: the assertive paragraph, the descriptive paragraph, and the narrative paragraph. This text will provide guided practice—lots of it—in several varieties of these paragraph forms.

2a   What Is an Assertive Paragraph?

In compositions, essay tests, short reports, and term papers, we find ourselves setting forth (or *asserting*) an idea and then supporting it as well as we can with examples and argument. The paragraphs used for this kind of writing are called *assertive paragraphs.* Since they are so common in college and career writing, assertive paragraphs should be mastered thoroughly.

Read the following assertive paragraph. Take careful note of the purpose of each inner division. Labels for the divisions appear in the margin.

[1] The *main idea* (or topic sentence)

[2] *Expansion* of the main idea

[3] *Illustration* (examples)

[4] *Conclusion* (answers the question, "So what?")

[1] In Brazil, a growing cottage industry converts the refuse of the middle class into items of necessity for the poor. [2] Urban garbage dumps provide a steady supply of tin cans, tires, and bottles for that new breed of Brazilian entrepreneur, the minimanufacturer. [3] Early each morning Manuel Ortiz visits Recife disposal areas to search out unbroken light bulbs. Stripped of their electrical elements, the glass shells become oil lamps for thousands of homes lacking electricity. In a neighboring village, Demetrio Santiz reclaims auto tires to fashion long-wearing sandals that retail for less than $1. [4] By such creative efforts, minimanufacturers have made a start at providing survival items for Brazil's growing poor.

Consider each inner division of the paragraph.

1. The *main-idea* sentence usually appears first in the paragraph. In this important position, it provides an *overview* of the rest of the paragraph.

2. The *expansion* sentence draws out the specific meaning of the main idea.
3. The *illustration* sentences provide examples that support the main idea.
4. The *conclusion* sentence (perhaps the most challenging sentence to write) brings the paragraph to a conclusion by answering the question, "*So what* if the main idea and illustration are true? *So what?*"

Now it is your turn. Locate each of the inner paragraph divisions within the following paragraph. (Write appropriate inner division labels in the left-hand margin.)

_____

_____

_____

_____

California geologists are gradually educating the tremor-prone state in a new language of earthquake measurement: the Mercalli Scale of Shock Intensities. Unlike the familiar Richter standard, the Mercalli Scale divides earthquake activity into twelve levels of intensity, as perceived by the public. A Level VI quake, for example, may be recognized by the ringing of church bells, the cracking of plaster, and the awakening of virtually all sleepers. In the days ahead, Californians will look less to the seismograph and more to their surroundings for a "reading" of earthquake intensity.

Exercise 2.1

In the following five paragraphs, supply the missing paragraph element. Notice that you are asked gradually to supply more and more of the paragraph until, in item 5, you are writing a complete assertive paragraph on your own.

1. The Homeowners' Association at Margate Condominiums refused to grant absolute freedom of interior design and decoration to owners. The association decided that any interior wall visible through an uncurtained window could not be painted or wallpapered in "distasteful or obnoxious colors." Purple and

(Illustration)

orange polka dots on the walls, for example, _____

_____ .

Homeowners fond of such hues have three choices: sue, move, or

buy curtains.

2. Americans have expanded the meaning of *family* to include pets of

(Expansion)   all varieties. _____

_____ . Aunt Mildred's fluffy poodle, for

(Illustration)   instance, _____

_____ .

While Americans may have fewer children than ever before,

"families" in the broad sense may be getting larger.

(Main idea)   3. _____

_____ .

(Expansion)   _____

_____ .

A majority of new homes in Arizona, for example, boast solar col-

lectors for heating water. Huge generator windmills have sprouted

on Hawaiian hilltops, providing electricity to dozens of village

(Conclusion—   homes. _____
answers "So
what?")   _____

_____ .

4. The plain uniforms worn by students in European secondary

schools help to ease some difficult social problems. _____

(Expansion)   _____

_____ .

(Illustration)   _____

_____ .

(Conclusion)   _____

_____ .

5. (You're on your own. Suggested topics are diets, beards, or chopsticks.)

_____

_____

_____

_____

_____

_____

_____

2a(1) Alternatives Variation

Any paragraph pattern, however useful, can become boring with constant repetition. Not every assertive paragraph follows the pattern described on the previous pages. In the *alternatives variation,* for example, the writer replaces the assertive paragraph's usual illustration section with two contrasting sentences, often beginning with the phrases *on the one hand* and *on the other hand.* Using this variation, you can demonstrate differences between two sets of ideas, facts, or observations. Notice in the following example how the illustration section is replaced by two contrasting sentences.

> Mystery surrounds the location of British steering wheels. Why should the English insist that driving on the right side of the road is, in fact, wrong? Roman and French invasions of England, on the one hand, should have instilled "right-thinking" as it is found on the Continent. On the other hand, such political imposition may have established native English eccentricities, including left-side driving, all the more firmly. Certainly the practice is here to stay; the rest of the world may have right and left, but England clings defiantly to left and wrong.

Similarly, alternatives can be signaled by the use of *but, however,* or *by contrast.*

> Most bats eat insects. But a rare variety, the fringe-lipped bat of Central America, makes a steady diet of live frogs.

Most bats eat insects. The fringe-lipped bat, by contrast, makes a steady diet of live frogs.

Most bats eat insects. The fringe-lipped bat, however, makes a steady diet of live frogs.

Exercise 2.2 | Insert appropriate alternatives in the spaces below. Signal the presence of the alternatives by using one or more of the following phrases: *on the one hand, on the other hand, but, however, by contrast.*

1. Prior to the advent of chemical and spectrographic analysis, pseudometeorites were the stock and trade of rural con-artists. Like snake oil and rain devices, heavy black stones, particularly those with an exotic streak of volcanic mottle, brought high prices. On the one hand, such stones _____

   _____

   _____ . On the other hand, _____

   _____

   _____ . Trusting purchasers often assigned these treasures an honored place on the mantle, where they were viewed with pride, awe, and not a little religious fear.

2. A Florida publisher marketed a little book of songs that could be played by pushing the appropriate buttons on a touch-tone telephone. The innocent amusement seemed _____

   _____

   _____ . Bell Telephone, _____ , _____

   _____

   _____ . Bell's advice, in short, was to let your fingers do the walking, but not the playing.

3. A curious set of emotions settles upon some people, perhaps

most, the day *after* they buy a new car. _____

(State alternative
emotions here.)

_____

_____

_____ . _____

_____

_____ . If the feelings persist, there is a

good chance that they will never be "driven" away.

2a(2) Series Variation

You may want to list several ideas, objects, or experiences in the course
of an assertive paragraph. This list is called a *series.* A good place to insert
a series into an assertive paragraph is in the slot usually held by the illustration. Introduce separate items in your series with such words as *first,*
second, and *finally.* Use a comma to set off such words from the rest of the
sentence.

> In a day when big magazines like *Look* and *Life* were folding, many
> small magazines found the back door to fortune. First, magazines like *Ski,*
> *Astronomy,* and *Hotrod* offered their advertisers an inexpensive way to
> reach a specialized audience. Second, such magazines relied on the
> freshness and creativity of free-lance writers for the bulk of their material.
> Finally, the small magazines found a place on the coffee tables of the
> "Me" generation as symbols of individuality and unusual interests.

Note that the conclusion sentence may often be omitted when writing the
series variation. The sentence beginning with *finally* has a conclusive ring
to it, and needs no further help.

Exercise 2.3

Insert the missing series in the space provided.

1. A high, barely perceived whine—whether from a lighting fixture or

a microphone—affects an audience in stages. First, _____

_____

(Describe a series
of audience
responses.)

_____

_____.

Second (or Then), _____

_____

_____.

Finally, _____

_____

_____.

(Describe the
stereotyped stages
of poor horror
films.)

2. Late night horror flicks all seem to proceed down the same worn

path. First, _____

_____

_____

_____. Second (or Then), _____

_____

_____

_____. Finally, _____

_____

_____.

3. (Your own series variation. Suggested topics are laziness, holiday

customs, inflation, or potato chips.)

(Remember to
begin with a main
idea.)

_____

_____

_____

_____

_____

_____

_____

_____

_____

_____

2a(3) If-Then Variation

Often one idea in your paragraph may depend on another idea in the way that an *effect* depends on a *cause.* The effect of icy roads, for example, depends on the *cause* of cold weather. We can express the relationship between the cause and effect by using an *if-then* sentence: "If the weather is cold tonight, then the roads will be icy." If-then sentences, of course, do not have to express only cause and effect relationships. Often, one fact is the *condition* for a following fact or event: "If the moon is full, then the ceremony can begin."

Such if-then sentences can be placed in the section of the assertive paragraph usually held by the illustration.

> Antiques have a special fascination for urban, industrialized society. The fluted, fringed creations of an earlier day soften life somehow. If the ivory-handled hair brush, the oak settee, or the mirrored mantel bring a hint of graciousness into the home, then the sterility of gypsum-board walls and shag carpets doesn't matter so much. Antiques are visual Valium.

Exercise 2.4 | Insert an appropriate if-then sentence in the space provided.

1. Early cathedral builders often worked on scale models before beginning actual construction. Delicate prototypes were built and tested for stress. If _____

   _____ , then _____

   _____

   _____ . The longevity of the massive structures bears eloquent witness to the essential soundness of their erectors' careful planning.

2. In personnel interviews, Supervisor Talbot claimed that he could see deeply into an interviewee's personality by watching the eyes. If _____

_____ , then _____

_____ .

Talbot finally had to be given other duties when he ceased reading files and resumes entirely, concentrating solely on the eyes, the eyes.

Recap

Review the following brief summary.

The Assertive Paragraph

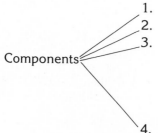

Components

1. Main idea (topic sentence)
2. Expansion (optional)
3. Illustration (examples)
   May be replaced with variations:
   On one hand, on the other hand
   First, second, finally
   If-then
4. Conclusion (So what?)

Review Test: Assertive Paragraphs

From the list below, select four topics and use them to write four assertive paragraphs. Model your paragraphs on the pattern summarized above. One paragraph should make use of illustration; the remaining three paragraphs should each employ one of the other variations listed.

Loopholes	Censorship	Leisure	Computers
Neighbors	Television	Obsession	Hats
Violence	Corporations	Summer Jobs	Roommates
Relationships	Discoveries	Welfare	Diets
Toys	Change	Boredom	Joy

Writing Topics: Assertive Paragraphs

The suggested writing topics that follow plunge you into situations: something is happening and someone needs to hear what you have to say. Keep in mind that these are *suggested* topics. You may, of course, make changes in the assignment in consultation with your instructor. Often, slight changes and adjustments will make writing the paragraph much more appealing to you.

1. A Cottage by the Sea

You decide to pool your savings with three friends so you can celebrate the Easter recess in style—with a week at the beach. Through a travel agent you rent, sight unseen, a cottage "only six blocks from the water's edge."

The cottage, to your delight, is clean and spacious. But although the water's edge is only blocks away, the nearest *public* access lies 6 miles down the highway. Large estates, all with fences and security alarms, occupy the rest of the oceanfront.

> Write one paragraph to the general public. Argue for the public's right to beach access.
> Write a second paragraph to the travel industry.* Argue for full disclosure in vacation advertising.
> Write a third paragraph to your friends. Suggest more careful investigation in the future.

2. Busted and Ready to Burst

You've had a great time visiting your best friend for a weekend at the university. But today you must fly home. On the way to the airport you both laugh as your friend's ancient VW sputters down the highway. Suddenly, just ahead, a late model Buick slams on its brakes to avoid hitting a puppy. Your friend brakes hard, but to no avail: you ram the back of the Buick. Its crumpled trunk springs open in the crash; as if in answer, the crushed hood of the VW flies up.

No one is hurt, not even the puppy. The driver of the Buick is a slight woman in her late forties, dressed primly in a dark blue suit. She holds the

---

Note: In this and all other assignments, let your assigned audience (in this case, travel agents) help you select appropriate examples and methods of argument. *Do not* cast your writing in the form of a letter. In real life, of course, many of these situations would call for writing a letter, not a paragraph. For now, however, we can use the situations to stimulate practice in the paragraph forms discussed in this chapter.

puppy in her arms as the police arrive. The officers listen to her story about the poor puppy, and then begin to inspect the damage. The larger of the two officers asks your friend several questions: "Were you following too closely? Is this old car registered? Where do you live?"

The other officer kneels down between the two cars and fetches a stuffed plastic bag from the pavement. He calls his partner over and they talk briefly. They approach you and your friend with handcuffs. The bag, it seems, contained the kind of grass you don't mow. One officer remarks that there must be $5,000 worth in the bag. Almost before you are able to speak coherently, both you and your friend find yourselves in the back of the patrol car, handcuffed, on your way to jail.

You are dumbfounded. Everything has happened so fast. You know for certain that *you* are innocent. Your friend swears innocence as well. The Buick drives off.

> Write one paragraph to the police. Protest against the injustice of judging from first appearances.
>
> Write a second paragraph to the general public. Point out how innocent citizens can become tangled in sticky legal situations.
>
> Write a third paragraph to your friend. Emphasize the importance of knowing the full truth about the matter.

3. The Burden of Fame

It has been only a year since Annuncio Valenza, the famous director, discovered your face—"What eyes! What character!"—behind the counter at McDonald's. What a year it has been! You have made two movies and innumerable public appearances. Now, with three weeks off, you sit with pen in hand, the waters of the Mediterranean lapping at your toes.

> Write a paragraph to your home-town friends. Assure them that you haven't changed. (Remember to write traditional essay paragraphs, not friendly letters.)
>
> Write a second paragraph to your fans. Tell them of your future artistic goals and plans.
>
> Write a third paragraph for a future autobiography. Discuss the trials and inconveniences of stardom.

4. Rally Around the Flag

A controversial bill is before the state legislature. It provides that all textbooks ordered by state-university professors be reviewed by a governmental committee. To receive the committee's approval, the books must be "in harmony with the true American beliefs and ideals we all cherish" and must "reflect a positive attitude toward the actions and policies of this great nation."

As a student at the state university, you are concerned that this bill will lead quickly to academic censorship.

Write one paragraph to legislators. Argue against the bill.

Write a second paragraph to the general public. Discuss the proper relationship between a university and the policies of a nation.

Write a third paragraph to fellow students. Describe the kind of censorship that could result from such a bill.

5. *Finally on the Map*

Your home town had looked forward to the extension of the interstate freeway as a boon to trade and tourism. But due to a last-minute planning change, the highway is now slated to cut an ugly swath right through historic Cypress Park. Four ornate turn-of-the-century civic buildings must be demolished.

Write one paragraph to state planners. Argue against the last-minute change in plans.

Write a second paragraph to the citizens of your home town. Arouse their support for Cypress Park and the civic buildings.

Write a third paragraph for the general public. Discuss the problems and perils that accompany progress.

Chapter 3
Writing Descriptive Paragraphs

3a What Is a Descriptive Paragraph?

Often, writers try to transfer to readers a mental picture of an object or scene. This process of transfer, of course, is known as *description,* and is carried out in descriptive paragraphs. Read the following descriptive paragraph. Try to determine three ways in which its inner divisions differ from those of the assertive paragraph. Write the differences in the space provided.

[1] During the bombings, the cathedral's huge rose window had been taken home piece by piece by the French villagers. [2] It stood restored now, except for a missing piece here and there. The vacant spots glared white in the morning sun, lost pieces memorializing lost lives. Tourists, say the villagers, love the window for what has been saved: its beautiful greens and blues and reds. [3] But the villagers love the window especially for the white—for what has been lost.

Differences

1. _____

2. _____

3. _____

As you may have concluded, the differences between the descriptive paragraph and the assertive paragraph are substantial. In the following sections, we will explore those differences one by one.

3a(1) The Approach Sentence

The descriptive paragraph replaces the topic sentence with an *approach sentence.* Unlike the topic sentence, the approach sentence doesn't try to provide an overview or summary of the paragraph's content. Its job is simply to set forth the approach or direction the writer wishes to maintain throughout the paragraph. Because it gives directional clues, the approach sentence is like an on-ramp to the descriptive paragraph. By reading the approach sentence, readers know from the beginning of the paragraph where they are headed. Notice how the following approach sentence establishes the direction for further description.

> Barbara eyed the mess on top of her dresser with disgust: a jumbled heap of yesterday's jewelry, orphaned mementoes, and half-forgotten photos.

Do you already have a feeling for the writer's approach? The paragraph will go on to treat several specific items on the dresser, such as the framed photo of Jerry Fornelli, grinning Jerry, now face down on the mahogany.

Exercise 3.1   For each of the topics below, write an approach sentence that could serve to begin a descriptive paragraph.

1. Christmas Shopping _____
   _____
   _____

2. A Storm _____
   _____
   _____

3. A Garden _____
   _____
   _____

4. A Statue _____
   _____
   _____

5. Night Noises _____

_____

_____

3a(2) Development

The middle portion, or *development,* of the descriptive paragraph presents specific details. Unlike the middle section of the assertive paragraph, the development does not break neatly into expansion and illustration segments. The phrase *for example,* so common in illustration, is often unnecessary in the descriptive paragraph where examples, after all, make up almost the entire paragraph.

Exercise 3.2   After each of the following approach sentences, continue the description by writing at least one sentence filled with specific details.

1. Her uncle's garage could hardly be described as "neat."

_____

_____

_____

2. An unusual tattoo spread across his bicep.

_____

_____

_____

3a(3) The Weighted Sentence

Finally, the descriptive paragraph concludes with a *weighted sentence.* It *may,* but does not have to, provide a summary for the paragraph after the fashion of the conclusion sentence. Almost always, however, the weighted sentence communicates special emphasis or significance.

Notice how the final weighted sentence sheds special light on Mr. Halston in the following paragraph. Not until the final sentence do we understand the feelings Mr. Halston attaches to his beautiful hair.

Halston's heavy, thick waves of blond hair hovered like a blessing on his head. We marveled that a man deep into middle age could still sprout such stuff. Without a part, the sunshine hairs cascaded this way and that, coyly covering half the ear and dallying in quarter-curls at the collar. Smart bangs covered, almost covered, the hint of fine webbing pasted high to his forehead. We noticed Halston sweating.

Exercise 3.3   Use the following approach sentence to begin a descriptive paragraph in which you develop specific details and then conclude with a weighted sentence (again, a sentence of special significance).

The crowd at the Fourth Street Auditorium waited for Mad Mikail and round one of "professional" wrestling. In front sat _____

_____

_____

_____

_____

_____

_____

In later exercises you will write more descriptive paragraphs. First, though, we should consider some simple techniques that make descriptive writing come alive.

3b Achieving Effective Description

3b(1) Choosing Details According to Your Purpose

A HANDY ANALOGY: Details are like flowers on a field. Pick the ones you *want;* don't try to harvest the whole lot.

But how do you know what details you want? Choose those that create the mood or make the case that you wish to communicate.

Exercise 3.4 Decide what you want to communicate to your reader about the game of pool: admiration or disgust. Then circle details in the following list that will help to reinforce your chosen attitude toward the game.

The appealing symmetry of the racked and ready balls

The heavy haze of rank cigarette smoke

The red and gold stained-glass lighting fixture

The smell of stale beer

The shrewd calculation of impacts and angles

The gentleman's code of "no noise while shooting"

Powdery cue chalk on fingers and clothes

The balance of the straight, varnished cue stick

The stupidity of putting balls in a hole with a stick

Stretched green felt, smooth to the touch

Idle boasts and lewd imprecations

Ever-changing challenges

A game for moles who never see the light of day

The satisfying "thunk" of the ball in the pocket

The game's long association with loafers and punks

The hot, white lights

The pleasing ebb and flow of tension and release

The false bravado of "studying the table"

The smart crack of the scattering balls

The absurd contortions as people try to reach for shots

A game of legends, such as that of Minnesota Fats

Look over the details you've chosen. You can understand the importance of *selecting* details according to some purpose or design. Just by your choice of details, you could make the game of pool out to be the sport of kings and counselors or the machination of the devil.

Exercise 3.5 In the exercises below, a purpose or design has been given. For each exercise, write at least one sentence containing details in keeping with the given purpose. The first item has been done for you as an example.

1. (You want to express your joy over the fact that it is finally raining.) Reaching up with petals and leaves, the flowers seem to celebrate the drops of rain.

2. (You want to describe a crowded beach.) _____

_____

_____

3. (You want to reflect how tired you are of classes.) _____

_____

_____

4. (The bakery tempts you.) _____

_____

_____

3b(2)   Including Sensory Details

Use details that stimulate the senses—sight, hearing, smell, taste, touch, and muscular movement. Reject bland generalizations. Try this simple test to determine if a word appeals to the senses: close your eyes, say the word, and decide if it activates any one of your senses. Do you see something in your mind's eye? Can you begin to hear or feel something?

Compare a bland generalization—

The man had some food and liked it.

with an alternative version filled with sensory details—

The soldier snapped the stale loaf in his bandaged hands. Puffing out bits of flaky crust between words, he grunted "Good, good."

Exercise 3.6 | In the list of words below, cross out those that do not stimulate a response from at least one of the senses.

gritty	whisper	good	dominant
crusty	gagging	babble	purr
superb	great	growl	tattered
shimmering	frosted	relevant	soaring
fuzz	radiant	stiff-lipped	strange
downy	stupid	lovely	dynamic
glossy	stretch	shriek	metallic
eagle-eyed	bitter	creamy	interrupt

Exercise 3.7 | For each of the bland generalizations below, write at least one sentence containing crisp, specific sense details.

1. The meal was good. _____

_____

2. The Superbowl was violent. _____

_____

3. Butilda is such a nice girl. _____

_____

4. The movie was gory. _____

_____

5. He had good looks but a poor personality. _____

_____

6. The tower was impressive. _____

_____

7. Nature is soothing. _____

_____

Exercise 3.8 | From wherever you find yourself sitting at this moment, look around and conjure up six sense words to describe your immediate surroundings.

_____ _____ _____ _____ _____ _____

Why do we bother to use sense words in description? In slight but tangible ways, our *bodies* respond to words and images evoking taste memories (*salty*), muscular strains (*twisted*), and other sensuous responses. An adventure novel full of chase scenes and physical peril, for example, can leave us with the sensation of physical effort, even exhaustion—"Whew! That was a *good* book!" By "good," in this case, we mean that we felt an involvement beyond mere rational understanding. We felt that we were there, and that the rotting floorboards endangering the book's characters were creaking beneath our feet as well. Only language that appeals to the senses can create this most powerful illusion in writing.

Exercise 3.9   Using one of the scenes below, write a descriptive paragraph that creates the sights, sounds, smells—in short, the actuality—of the event as you imagine it.

1. Football players pile one after another on top of the hapless quarterback. Describe what the quarterback feels at the bottom of the pile.

   _____

   _____

   _____

   _____

   _____

   _____

   _____

   _____

2. After a six-week diet of carrots, grapefruit, water, and cheese, Marlene lets go at an ice-cream parlor. Describe her sensations as she decides what, and how many, items to order.

   _____

   _____

   _____

   _____

   _____

   _____

_____

_____

_____

3. Frank fancies himself an auto mechanic, and is determined to replace his VW transmission by himself. Unfortunately, he lacks the proper tools and tries to make do with an old pair of pliers and an adjustable wrench. Picture him on his back under the car, his frustration building. Describe his growing exasperation. (You might consider describing the effects on knuckles, hair, eyes, and so forth.)

_____

_____

_____

_____

_____

_____

_____

_____

4. Kristi tries each of the samplers at the perfume counter. The exotic scents transport her to different realms of sensation, imagination, and memory. Invent names for three perfumes, then describe in sense terms Kristi's brief reveries as she tries a spray of each.

_____

_____

_____

_____

_____

3b(3) **Establishing a Pattern**

Establish a pattern for description. Don't wander. All good descriptive paragraphs have some internal pattern of organization—a path that guides both writer and reader.

Let's say, for example, that a novelist wants to describe the city of Cincinnati just at the break of dawn. She recognizes that a whole library of books could be written in an effort to catalog all the details of such a scene. So she wisely *selects* details appropriate to her purpose. But she is still left with a dilemma: how are those details best arranged? By establishing a pattern of organization, she arranges her details into an effective order. Here is the paragraph she produces.

> Cincinnati yawns with the opening of big factory doors, huge swinging slabs of sheet metal and iron. The city grumbles with the coughing ignition of a thousand engines, then wheezes out a whistle here and there: "time to work." Faster now, the growls lose themselves in the hiss of transport tires on wet asphalt. A chorus of cheap spoons clink in yellowed coffee mugs, and telephones answer. Cincinnati, awake now, hears the hum and hustle of its heart, and does not smile.

Try to describe the pattern of organization that connects together all the details in this paragraph.

_____

_____

_____

We will now investigate several of the patterns you may choose to use in organizing your descriptive paragraphs. To begin with, be aware that nature offers at least two general organizing patterns: space and time. After all, the natural objects (people, places, and things) that fill our descriptive paragraphs all have a place in the order of things in space and time. We can use this natural order as a pattern for organizing description.

The Space Pattern: Near to Far

In the near-to-far pattern of organization, deal first with details close to you (or to a person in your paragraph). Gradually draw in details that are farther and farther away.

> Close to her forehead, now brushing it, Jeanette felt the cling of an ancient spider web. Beyond, cold and small in the darkness, a single candle flickered.

Exercise 3.10 | Use the pattern of near to far in describing the following scene. Begin with an approach sentence, develop your description, then conclude with a weighted sentence.

(Madam D'Arcy looks out upon the grounds of her palatial estate.)

_____

_____

_____

_____

_____

_____

_____

The Space Pattern: Side to Side

Arrange your details as they appear from one side to the other.

> To the right of the field stood the knights, rigid and proud in their burnished battle-ware. Stretched in clots across the center grass were townspeople, only half aware of the impending struggle. And far to the left, alone, wandered a festooned clown.

Exercise 3.11 | Use a side-to-side pattern in describing the following scene.

(Fran looks around the gymnasium at her first high school dance.)

_____

_____

_____

_____

_____

_____

_____

_____

The Space Pattern: Small to Large

Organize your details in the order of their physical size.

> Janson dusted gingerly at the crusted finger of metal now exposed against the red earth. With an hour's digging, the finger became a latch, the latch brought a lid, and finally an ancient chest lay fully exposed to view. Janson steadied himself and breathed deeply. Open it, a hundred voices shouted within him.

Exercise 3.12   Use a small-to-large (or large-to-small) pattern to organize your details about the following scene. Write an approach sentence, a development section, and a weighted sentence.

(Tricia redecorates her apartment using only shades of red.)

_____

_____

_____

_____

_____

_____

_____

_____

The Time Pattern: Moment to Moment

Look out a window from where you now sit. If there are no windows, imagine a forest scene. Each object upon which your eye falls is separated from other objects not only by space but also by *time*. You, after all, saw one object *before* the next. Almost as if giving a slide show, *you* determine the time sequence in which objects pass before your view. Object A may get a moment, object B a mere second, and object C an hour of concentration. Time thus becomes a *path* that orders the arrangement and importance of details.

The simplest and most natural time pattern arranges one detail after another in the order, moment by moment, that they caught your attention. Another name for this pattern is *chronological order*.

In the following example, notice how we see details as Donna sees them, moment by moment.

> Famished after her unexpected trek, Donna let her eyes run riot in the marketplace of the village. Surrounding her were baskets of tangerines and apples, trays of dates and sliced breadfruit, and papayas as large as a person's head. She reached for a guava, only to meet the challenging stare of a pot-bellied merchant. He thrust a brown, pudgy hand in her face, palm up.

Exercise 3.13 Organize a descriptive paragraph about the scene below according to the way details follow one after the other. Include an approach sentence, a development section, and a final weighted sentence.

(While waiting downtown for a friend, you wander into a pet shop. Describe your impressions and sensations as you move about the store.)

_____

_____

_____

_____

_____

_____

_____

_____

The Time Pattern: Flashback

Often our perception of objects does not follow moment-to-moment order. When, let's say, we wander about the pet shop of the previous exercise, one item, a puppy perhaps, may stimulate memories from the past. We "flash back" to the early scene, then return again to the present moment.

> Toni surveyed the spilled jewelry box. Stupid cat! Her eye fell on earrings she hadn't worn in years—precious little gold studs with almost invisible diamond chips. But they had meant the world that night at the prom. Her mind whirled back, back into a montage of taffeta, heady perfume, moist palms, and a tall boy in a baggy white dinner jacket. She held the earrings in her hand for a long moment. Then carefully, watching herself in the mirror, she put them in her ears.

Exercise 3.14 | In describing the following scene, break out of moment-to-moment time to flash back to an earlier set of details. Write a full descriptive paragraph.

(Maxine watches her four-year-old nephew splash in a wading pool. Her mind drifts back to a previous moment in her own life.)

_____

_____

_____

_____

_____

_____

_____

_____

Before dealing with two final patterns for the organization of descriptive detail, let's sum up the patterns discussed so far.

Space Patterns	Time Patterns
Near to far	Moment to moment
Side to side	Flashback
Small to large	

Exercise 3.15 | Choose one of the physical paths above to order details about the following scene. Write a complete descriptive paragraph.

(Harry Burnell, desperately afraid of flying, experiences his own private hell as he takes off in a 747.)

_____

_____

_____

_____

_____

_____

_____

_____

The Analogy Pattern

An analogy is a comparison in which less familiar ideas or circumstances are compared to more familiar ideas or circumstances. The result is clearer understanding. A distant galaxy, with its arm-like swirls of stars, can be described using the analogy of a pinwheel. Your ancestors, similarly, can be conveniently held in mind by means of the family *tree.*

When a writer spells out a comparison in detail through the course of a descriptive paragraph, he or she is using *analogy* as a path for organizing details.

> Grandmother Keefe looked through the spattered windshield. Dotted white lines perforated the ribbon of black asphalt stretching on and on before her across the prairie. The stuttering lines reminded her ever so much of stitches, all neat, on and on. She looked back at the farm once. Grasping the wheel, she felt like sewing. Her car became her Singer, and she told herself to crazy-quilt her way, some way.

Exercise 3.16 | Learn to create analogies by drawing a line from one experience in column A to an item in column B. Since many combinations are possible, select the matching pair that interests you most. Feel free to substitute your own combinations. "Getting engaged," for example, may be comparable to "stepping to the edge of an abyss."

A	B
Summer jobs	Arteries and veins
A visit to the dentist	Judgment Day
Getting engaged	A pineapple
Freeways	Traversing a mine field
Sleeplessness	Buying a laundromat
Final examinations	Slow dripping of water

Exercise 3.17 Now write a descriptive paragraph based on the analogy you chose above. State your analogy (the items to be compared) in your approach sentence at the beginning of the paragraph. Develop the analogy by specifying at least three ways in which the item from column A is similar to the selected item in column B. Conclude with an appropriate weighted sentence.

_____

_____

_____

_____

_____

_____

_____

_____

The Emotion Pattern

Our feelings color our view of objects and events. By selecting a particular emotion, a writer can create a pattern by which to choose and arrange the details of descriptive paragraphs. Notice how an emotional mood determines the details making up this description of a hopeless moment.

The fourth night he knew: help would not come. The Arctic wind still howled past the quaking nylon tent, but now it was talking to someone else. Sinclair stuffed himself deeper into the goose-down bag.

Against his nose, catching at the stubble on his chin, the bag still smelled new, plastic. Now he was writing a check for $168.32 to Culver Mountain Outfitters. And he was going to speak to the man he knew at the store, to Mike. But he needed to catch his breath. He shifted and felt his boots, heavy and wet, wedged down at the narrow bottom of the bag. He knew he could sleep but that he shouldn't, shouldn't and could, and must not, but could. He would.

How different the details of this paragraph would be if Sinclair felt optimistic that help would arrive in time.

Exercise 3.18 "Rescue" Sinclair by writing a descriptive paragraph beginning with the faint drone of an airplane. As he rouses himself with new hope, choose details in keeping with his brightening spirits.

_____

_____

_____

_____

_____

_____

_____

_____

_____

Exercise 3.19 In columns A, B, and C below, three emotional patterns are set forth. Along the left side are three experiences. By filling in the blanks, demonstrate how the details of each experience are determined by each emotional path in columns A, B, and C. An example is provided.

	A. Elated	*B. Frightened*	*C. Angry*
Blind date	fascinating conversation	strange looks	piggish manners
	(detail)		
	_____	_____	_____
	(detail)		

	A. Elated	B. Frightened	C. Angry
	_____	_____	_____
	_____	_____	_____
Job interview	_____	_____	_____
	_____	_____	_____
	_____	_____	_____
Walking alone at night	_____	_____	_____
	_____	_____	_____
	_____	_____	_____

Recap

Review the following brief summary.

The Descriptive Paragraph
1. Approach sentence
2. Development   Components
3. Weighted sentence

Keys to Powerful Description
1. Select details
2. Show details that stimulate senses
3. Establish a pattern for details
   The space pattern
      Near to far
      Side to side
      Small to large
   The time pattern
      Moment to moment
      Flashback
   The analogy pattern
   The emotion pattern

Review Test: Descriptive Paragraphs

Now choose three of the following topics. For each, write a descriptive paragraph making use of one of the patterns above. Try not to use the same pattern twice.

1. How the World Appears from the Top of a Mountain or Tall Building
2. A Used-Car Lot
3. An Art Gallery
4. A City Dump
5. A Picnic
6. A Favorite Lake, Beach, or Other Recreation Area
7. A Piece of Jewelry
8. Fireworks
9. Twilight
10. A Storm

Writing Topics: Descriptive Paragraphs

1. Grandma's Attic

You volunteered to clean out your grandmother's attic. You had no way of knowing, however, that a chaos of hat boxes, Christmas lights, old toasters, and general clutter would confront you, surround you, in the dusty light. One large trunk catches your eye. It lies open. A stack of photographs, old but still clear, begs to be dusted off.

> Write a paragraph in which you describe the world you see in those photographs. Write as if your words were to be part of a family history.
>
> Write a second paragraph to the general public. Reflect upon change.
>
> Write a paragraph as if it were for your journal. Describe how your grandmother looked when she was your age.

You may want to review Chapter 3 before beginning to write paragraphs on the topics below. Chapter 3 explains the importance of using sense details and following a descriptive pattern.

2. Bon Appetit!

Your part-time job with the local newspaper has worked out well. The editor likes your style. In fact, she says, you are ready to write a weekly restaurant review for the paper.

Write a paragraph for the general public. Describe a particularly pleasurable eating experience.

Write a paragraph, again for the general public. Describe an absolutely disastrous restaurant outing.

Write a paragraph to your editor. Describe the kinds of bribes you have been offered by restaurateurs seeking a good review.

3. Up, Up, and Away

The hot-air balloon looked lovely from a distance: an inverted tear drop floating huge above the landscape. Once inside the wicker basket, you could see and smell the inner workings of the miracle. The pilot gave a tug on the burner control, driving hot air into the massive nylon bag.

Write a paragraph to nonballoonists. Describe your sensations on your first lift-off.

Write a second paragraph for your own journal. Describe what you saw and felt once the flight was under way.

Write a third paragraph to the pilot who took you up for the first time. Describe both your moments of exhilaration and your twinges of nervousness.

4. Things That Go Bump in the Night

You had had the opportunity of a lifetime. Your sister, a botanist, was going to investigate butterflies in the dense jungles of West Africa. She had invited you to assist her.

Now, in the blackness of your tent more than 70 miles from civilization, you lie awake.

Write a paragraph to the general public. Describe the night sounds you hear.

Write a second paragraph for your travel diary. Describe the personal feelings aroused by the strange sounds in the night.

Write a paragraph as if it were for a travel magazine. Select one particular sound. Describe it in careful detail, suggesting other more familiar sounds that it reminds you of.

5. Home Is Where the Heart Is

You didn't like the apartment when you first rented it, and you don't like it now. You daydream about the perfect dwelling place.

> Write a paragraph to the general public. Describe the home of your dreams.
>
> Write a second paragraph as if it were for your journal. Focus on three details in your dream home, explaining their importance.
>
> Write a third paragraph for others who hate their living spaces. Describe little things that can be done to brighten up an otherwise bleak apartment or house.

Chapter 4
Writing Narrative Paragraphs

4a What Is a Narrative Paragraph?

Our lives are full of action. The effort to capture a sense of movement, activity, and happening in words is called *narrative writing.* For many writers, the narrative paragraph is a close cousin to the descriptive paragraph. Notice, for example, that the narrative paragraph often follows the same pattern of organization as the descriptive paragraph.

[1] Approach sentence	[1] Masley had locked his keys in the car by himself, and he resolved to get them out by himself. [2] He jammed a crooked piece of coat hanger through the rubber door seal, telling himself that the ripped rubber would hardly be noticed. Fishing the wire about ever so carefully, he succeeded, after fifteen minutes, in dropping the hanger through onto the car seat. Masley pondered his next attempt. Finding a rusty nail on the pavement, he set to picking the door lock from the outside. He pushed and pried the nail back and forth. A loud click made Masley grin with satisfaction.
[2] Development	
[3] Weighted sentence	[3] He pulled out the nail—or most of it; the tip had broken off inside the still locked door.

In this chapter, we will apply several of the paragraph patterns we have already discussed to the writing of narrative paragraphs.

Exercise 4.1 Complete the following narrative paragraph by writing the development portion and the weighted sentence. The approach sentence has been provided.

The old circus performer put aside his forebodings and stepped out onto the highwire. _____

(Development) _____

_____

_____

_____

_____

_____

_____

(Weighted
sentence)   _____

_____

    In developing the paragraph in Exercise 4.1, you may have borrowed patterns from descriptive paragraphs. Perhaps you followed a time pattern and told, moment to moment, what happened to the old performer. You may have chosen the emotion pattern, tracing the man's feelings as he tested his weight on the wire. Perhaps you flashed back to an earlier, happier time in his life and circus career. All of these patterns are suitable for the writing of narrative paragraphs. Before exploring several such patterns in depth, let's investigate two keys to powerful narrative writing.

4b   Achieving Effective Narration

4b(1)   Using the Active Voice

Active narration ("the bear <u>smashed</u> the food locker") is generally more effective than *passive* narration ("the food locker <u>was smashed</u> by the bear"). In active narration, *actors* (such as lions, students, or swimmers) perform *actions* (such as roar, study, or plunge). Develop your skill in active narration in the following exercise.

Exercise 4.2 | Convert each of the following sentences to active narration (in which actors perform action). An example is shown.

The space debris was approached by the satellite.

The satellite approached the space debris.

1. The tennis tournament was won by the Australian.

   _____

   _____

2. Nine languages were spoken by the countess's secretary.

   _____

   _____

3. The topsoil was scoured away by the raging winds.

   _____

   _____

4. An experimental drug was prescribed by the young physician.

   _____

   _____

5. The efforts of the firefighters were applauded by the anxious crowd.

   _____

   _____

You will find further practice in active voice on page 60 of this text.

4b(2)   Choosing Vivid Verbs

When narrating action, select verbs (action words) that create vivid pictures (and sometimes sounds). Notice that "The lame pony went down the path" is less vivid than "The lame pony hobbled down the path." Vivid verbs such as *hobbled* speak directly to the senses. You can close your eyes and seem to see or smell or taste or feel a vivid verb. Colorless verbs, by contrast, carry only their dictionary meanings to you. They do not arouse your senses. In the following exercise, practice converting colorless verbs to vivid verbs.

Exercise 4.3 | Circle the colorless verbs in the sentences below. Then rewrite the sentences, replacing the circled verbs with vivid verbs appealing to the senses, as shown in the example.

> The cuckoo clock (fell) to the pavement below.
> The cuckoo clock crashed to the pavement below.

1. A warm breeze came through the pine trees.

   _____

   _____

2. The heavy tractor drove down the narrow cobbled lanes.

   _____

   _____

3. Blushing, the actress held the huge bouquet in her arms.

   _____

   _____

4. The weary back packers walked up the last mile of switchback trail to the summit.

   _____

   _____

5. Six frantic pigeons ate the bread crumbs from my hand.

   _____

   _____

4b(3)   Establishing a Pattern

The Space Pattern: Far to Near

Action often begins far from you and moves closer. You can pattern narrative paragraphs, like descriptive ones, after this movement of far to near (or near to far, side to side, up to down, and so forth). In the following example, notice how the actions of a marching band develop as the music moves from far to near.

Far to the east we glimpsed the marching band cresting Founder's Hill. At first just a red and white postage stamp, the square of color spread larger and larger as it edged down Sixth Avenue. We heard a distant tweedle, rattle, thump, and sunlight flared off cymbals and bobbing tubas. Growing wider now, filling the avenue, the band fanned out into ranks and files. Scottish drums told upon our stomachs, and trumpets shrilled in our ears. The band was upon us.

Notice that details are organized (or patterned) according to the space pattern of far to near. From afar, the band appears only as a "red and white postage stamp" to the eyes. The band's music, from afar, is a "distant tweedle." But details change dramatically as the band moves closer. The ranks and files of the marchers become visible. The drums and trumpets are no longer a distant noise but now make themselves felt in the stomach and ears. Practice such far to near narration in the following exercise.

Exercise 4.4 | Complete the following paragraph, arranging narrative details in the space pattern of far to near. The approach sentence is given for you.

On the horizon appeared the president's campaign train, a short gray line against the distant green fields. _____

(Development) _____

_____

_____

_____

_____

_____

_____

(Weighted sentence) _____

_____

The Time Pattern: Moment to Moment

Like moment-to-moment descriptive writing, narration often develops according to the pattern of moment-to-moment time (or chronological order). The narration of a horse race, for example, might begin with the starting gun, proceed around the track as time ticks away, and conclude at the finish line. Similarly, the narration of a chick hatching might begin with the first quiet pecks against the shell; then the larger pieces split off; and finally the bedraggled chick emerges. Sentences in such narrative writing are often linked by transition words such as *first, second, then, next, later,* and *finally.* Not all of these transition words, of course, would appear in the same paragraph.

Exercise 4.5

Give a moment-to-moment pattern to the narrative paragraph you're about to write. Remember to use active, vivid verbs. In the paragraph, narrate the precise actions of a sports star, as you imagine them, during the last few minutes prior to a championship match.

(Approach
sentence)   _____

                   _____

(Development)   _____

                   _____

                   _____

                   _____

                   _____

                   _____

                   _____

                   _____

                   _____

(Weighted
sentence)   _____

                   _____

The Analogy Pattern

Often one set of actions—what happens on the first day on a new job, let's say—may bring to mind another, comparable set of occurrences from a different realm—perhaps being lost in the woods. When you find two sets of action that seem alike even though they are different in kind, you've found an *analogy:* two essentially dissimilar experiences (starting the job, for example, and wandering, lost, in the woods) that have several similar aspects (the sensation of being lost, the many possible ways to proceed, and so forth). Analogies are useful to the narrative writer, just as they are to the descriptive writer. When the writer compares an unfamiliar experience to a familiar experience by means of an analogy, the reader understands more easily.

Consider two examples of narrative analogies:

Betting on horses *is analogous to* throwing coins into a wishing well.

How so? Probably you understand that betting on horses often reflects the same kind of naive wishing that throwing coins into a wishing well does. In both cases, money is usually thrown away.

Summer vacation *is analogous to* finding an escalator after three flights of stairs.

If the school year can be compared to climbing stairs, then summer vacation can seem like an effortless ride. Practice your own analogies in the following exercise.

Exercise 4.6 | Create analogies for each of the items listed.

1. Working on a hot, muggy summer day *is analogous to* _____

   _____

2. Starting a new diet *is analogous to* _____

   _____

3. Jogging *is analogous to* _____

   _____

4. Getting a new pet *is analogous to* _____

   _____

5. Christmas shopping *is analogous to* _____

   _____

Narrative paragraphs developed according to the pattern of analogy often follow a "First, Then (or Second), and Finally" scheme. Notice how these words provide links between sentences in the following example.

Large cocktail parties are like a vast roulette wheel. *First,* the whole affair is set spinning to the music: bright party dresses whirl among jaunty sports jackets. *Then* the serious business of socializing begins. Like a roulette ball, an individual circles the spinning crowd. The lonely ball waits, watching for a niche—a place to fit in, an interesting face. *Finally,* with a click, the roulette ball finds its slot on the wheel. The party spins on. Next?

Exercise 4.7

Complete the following narrative paragraph, using the pattern of analogy. The approach sentence is given for you.

(Development)

Reading a good book is like visiting a friend. First, _____

_____

_____ . Then _____

_____ .

(Weighted sentence)

Finally, _____

_____

_____ .

Exercise 4.8

Narrate a description of the bustle on campus during the first week of school. Suggestion: To find a suitable analogy, try this approach: "The first week of school reminds me of _____ ." Once you have filled in the blank, your paragraph can go on to explore specific ways in which your analogy holds true. State your analogy in the approach sentence.

(Approach sentence)

_____

_____

(Development)

_____

_____

_____

(Weighted
sentence)

_____

_____

_____

_____

_____

_____

Recap

Review the following brief summary.

The Narrative Paragraph
1. Approach sentence
2. Development ——————— Components
3. Weighted sentence

Keys to Effective Narration
1. Use the active voice
2. Choose vivid verbs
3. Establish a pattern
    The space pattern
      Far to near (and others)
    The time pattern
      Moment to moment (and others)
    The analogy pattern

Review Test: Narrative Paragraphs

Choose three of the following topics. For each, write a narrative
paragraph making use of one of the patterns discussed in this chapter.
Try not to use the same pattern twice.

1. A sleepless night
2. Moving
3. Paying bills

4. Studying past midnight
5. Wearing tight shoes
6. Babysitting
7. Writing a paragraph
8. Taking off in an airplane
9. Driving during rush hour traffic
10. Feeling drowsy in class

Writing Topics: Narrative Paragraphs

You may find it helpful to review Chapter 4 before beginning to write on these topics. Chapter 4 discusses the use of the active voice, vivid verbs, and a suitable paragraph pattern.

1. Speaking Habits

As a congressional aide to Senator Brenton Wheeler, you stand present in the wings as the senator delivers a television address. Although his words make sense because you wrote the speech, his speaking habits—gestures, voice, pauses, eye contact, and all the rest—make you shudder. The speech flops badly.

> Write a paragraph to a friend, narrating the problems that developed as the senator spoke.
>
> Write a paragraph to the senator, responding to his request for constructive criticism of his speaking habits.
>
> Write a paragraph for your private office journal. Narrate the actions you plan to take as the senator's aide to improve his speaking habits.

2. Horses

As a historian, you have long been fascinated—obsessed, your critics say—with the role of the horse in American history.

> Write a paragraph for your soon-to-be-published college history textbook. Narrate the actions of "the most important horse in

American history prior to 1900." (Make up any necessary facts, people, places, and events. Your critics will never know.)

Write a paragraph for your soon-to-be-published editorial, "New Uses for the Horse in Modern America." Narrate several activities in which horses might conceivably play a role. Your editorial will be read by the general public.

Write a paragraph for your soon-to-be-published autobiography, *Side-saddle.* Narrate the events that led to your fascination with the horse. Your autobiography will be read by the general public—if it is read at all.

3. The Longest Minutes

Late on a Friday afternoon you walk into the lobby of the Central National Bank to deposit a paycheck. Just as you approach the teller's window, three masked robbers burst through the door. Before you can decide what to do, you feel a rough hand pushing you away from the window.

Write a paragraph for your journal or diary. Narrate the events during the robbery, the longest minutes of your life.

Write a paragraph for the police department. Tell what happened in as clear and orderly a way as you can.

Write a third paragraph for the general public. Tell your version of the robbery.

4. Prime Time

Does TV violence influence the behavior of children? A major television network has hired you to find the answers. You have labored long and hard on the project, and have spent a great deal of the network's money. You think you have an answer.

Write a paragraph to network executives. Narrate the major steps you undertook in your study.

Write a paragraph for parents. Narrate several actions they can take in the home to make TV safe for their children.

Write a paragraph for a professional journal. Narrate the behavior of Tommy, a child deeply influenced by a steady diet of TV violence.

5. Coach

More than five hundred friends attended your retirement banquet. They helped you celebrate the end of a coaching career that spanned college and professional positions. You won more than you lost—far more.

> Write a paragraph for a sports magazine. Narrate the three most difficult, but most satisfying, actions you took over the years as a coach.
>
> Write a paragraph for your memoirs. Narrate the most heart-breaking event in your life in sports.
>
> Write a paragraph for youngsters. Narrate the actions they can take in their early years to build confidence and ability in sports.

Chapter 5
Writing with Style

5a What Is Style?

Below, four students discuss what it means to "write with *style*." Put a check by the opinion that accords with your own. If you disagree with all four students, write out your own opinion in the space provided.

JAN FORRESTER: Writing with style means having a lot of, well, pizzazz—something really unique or artsy about the way you express yourself.

BILL CONNELLY: Writing with style means following a style manual or grammar book accurately. If you don't make grammar mistakes, your writing has proper style.

CRAIG BRELLIS: In my opinion, the concept of "writing with style" involves the differentiation between intellectual diction and common words. Only by augmenting one's vocabulary can one attain style in written expression.

BRENDA LARSON: Writing with style just means being yourself, letting go. We each have our own unique style, you know, and each of us is important. Being sincere, that's what it means to write with style.

YOUR OPINION: _____

_____

_____

_____

_____

Perhaps we can better understand what style *is* by observing what it is *not.* Force yourself to read through the following paragraph. Rarely will you find so many different stylistic problems in one place. Each of these problems is numbered and, one by one, these errors will be explained and solved in the coming pages. Then, at the end of the chapter, you will have the opportunity to rewrite the paragraph, repairing its many flaws.

Police Chief and Daily Times *Feud Over Dageford Case*

[1] Yesterday the decision that was made by the police chief was to defend his officers against all charges in the Dageford case. [2] The response that was made by the *Daily Times* was to challenge the chief to make all files public on the matter. [3] And as a result [4] this caused [5] irritation on the part of the chief. Here are the facts. Two officers arrested Dageford, editor of the *Daily Times,* for running a red light on June 14. They [6] read him his rights, were securing him to the steering wheel with handcuffs, and then the alleged verbal berating of the arrested man began. [7] One would think that you could use less force in such an arrest. [8] They were [9] laying it on rather thick. [10] Let us underline the point that Dageford [11] didn't show any am't. of resistance [12] (the officers said he struggled violently). [13] What happened next? Dageford's [14] involuntary detention in full public view was prolonged for more than an hour while the officers questioned him. [15] The officers questioned him, Dageford claims, to embarrass the *Daily Times.* The officers and the chief have no comment on Dageford's charges.

This awful hodgepodge contains no overt spelling or grammatical errors. The passage, in fact, has its share of big words and long sentences. Apparently the writer's sentiments are sincere. Why, then, do we feel something akin to nausea when we plod through the wretched piece?

It lacks style.

Jonathan Swift's definition of good style is direct: "Proper words in proper places." But what does *proper* mean? How do we know when we have located the "proper" word in the "proper" place? In the space provided below, suggest ways you can determine *which* words belong *where* when you write.

_____

_____

_____

_____

_____

Now think about your methods for determining the proper places for the proper words in light of the following forces that act upon our sense of style.

1. *Common sense.* We know enough not to cut butter with an ax. What *can* be said simply *should* be said simply.
2. *Sensitivity to our readers.* What can they be expected to make from our words? To what extent should we consider their interests and abilities in choosing what to say and how to say it?
3. Our *grasp of what it is, after all, that we want to say.*
4. Our *knowledge of what can and can't be done in the English language.* By stretching the language, we may be able to "thumify the slidipy," that is, invent a few of our own spellings and definitions. But language has boundaries. If we cwriex tihwo cgpte, communication ceases. The boundaries of English grammar have been crossed, and we are no longer within the English language.
5. Our *love of variety*—in sound, sense and image—and our boredom with meaningless repetition.

This chapter will provide "hands-on" exercises in fifteen matters of style that bear on college and career writing. Through these exercises, you can learn to recognize and correct major stylistic errors.

A Menu of Fifteen Matters of Style
1. Using the active voice
2. Varying sentence types
3. Emphasizing important words through placement
4. Being specific
5. Eliminating wordiness
6. Creating parallels
7. Choosing pronouns
8. Controlling paragraph length
9. Avoiding trite and slang expressions
10. Avoiding a posed and overwritten style
11. Avoiding contractions and abbreviations
12. Using parentheses correctly
13. Avoiding unnecessary questions
14. Choosing words carefully
15. Avoiding awkward constructions and repetitions

5b   Using the Active Voice

In Section 4b(1) we introduced the importance of using the active voice. Readers of English want to know *who* did *what*? Satisfy that basic desire by beginning your sentences with an *actor* (or subject). Let an appropriate *action* follow without delay.

NOT: The grasslands were swept by the prairie fire.

INSTEAD: The prairie fire swept across the grasslands.

         Actor   *Action*

Exercise 5.1 | Convert the weak, wandering sentences below into direct, efficient sentences in which actors do action.

1. The antique brass knobs were installed by the cabinet maker.

_____

_____

_____

2. It was the Welsh Corgi that won the contest.

_____

_____

_____

3. The cabin was crushed by the massive tree.

_____

_____

_____

4. The fog was pierced by the bright halogen lights.

_____

_____

_____

5. There were three padlocks securing the door.

_____

_____

_____

6. The geraniums were eaten by the goats.

_____

_____

_____

7. The show is being seen by people across the world.

_____

_____

_____

8. His hat was doffed by the proper old gentleman.

_____

_____

_____

9. The Ming vase was broken by Cousin Billy.

_____

_____

_____

10. Wool suits were often worn by even the younger generation.

_____

_____

_____

Notice the effect of the changes you made in the foregoing exercise. Colorless verbs, such as *was, were, is,* and *are,* moved over for action verbs like *crushed, pierced,* and *doffed.* Readers delight in finding vivid, lively action at the heart of your writing.

Exercise 5.2 | In the blanks provided, write down verbs that describe action.

_____freeze_____   _____

_____uncover_____   _____

_____   _____

_____   _____

Action verbs lose their liveliness if they are encumbered by too many auxiliary, or "helper," verbs, such as *is* and *was.* Observe the change from the strong, action form,

The compressor crumples the old car.

to the encumbered form,

The compressor is crumpling the old car.

Whenever possible, let action verbs express themselves in their most direct form, without the barnacles of helper verbs.

Exercise 5.3 | Convert each encumbered action verb below to its most direct form:

is yielding   _____

was approaching   _____

were tittering   _____

are releasing   _____

As a general rule, at least half of your verbs should be active. When the colorless forms *is, are, was, were, has, have* and *seems to be* dominate your writing, your prose may sound too much like an insurance contract or a tax manual. Action verbs create an energetic style.

Writers who depend too much on *is, are, was,* and *were* often suffer from a frustrating form of "writer's block." Since *is* functions as an equals sign (=), such writers are forever seeking *equivalence* relationships for their subjects. Take a horse, for example: an "is" writer seeks to state what a horse *is* or *equals* and, so, ends up with such stuff as, "A horse *is* a four-legged creature that. . . ." How much easier it is to seek action relationships. We can call to mind dozens of actions (jump, trot, canter, gallop) for a horse. By contrast, we often hit a difficult block when we force ourselves to state what a horse *is*, a corporation *is*, or a baby *is*.

Certainly, *is*, *are*, *was*, and *were* should not disappear from our writing. We should, however, rely on action verbs for our most common sentences.

Exercise 5.4 | Rewrite the following paragraph, converting colorless verb forms into action verbs wherever possible and appropriate.

> Discouragement was felt by the basketball players as the halfway point in the season was nearing. If lack of talent had been the problem for the players, the disappointment of losing seven out of nine games would have been something that could have been borne. But the truth was known by every player: the problem was Coach Riley. The team was forced by him to run plays and patterns that were outdated. The plays were called "classic" by Coach Riley, but they were called "antique" by the players and their opponents.

_____

_____

_____

_____

_____

_____

_____

_____

_____

_____

In the preceding paragraph, you have changed passive verbs to active verbs. The passive verb form specifies that an action was performed *by* someone or something, though often the agent is not stated (as in "The task was begun."). Repeated use of passive verbs can rob your writing of immediacy and energy. Compare, for example, the passive construction,

> The trout was caught by Harrison.

with the active version,

> Harrison caught the trout.

In our mind's eye, we can visualize an actor performing an action more vividly than we can picture an object having an action performed upon it by someone or something.

Unless you have strong cause to maintain the passive form, regularly choose the actor-action pattern.

Exercise 5.5   Revise the following sentences so that the unnecessary passive verb forms are restated as active forms.

1. A speech was made by the chairperson.

   _____

   _____

   _____

2. The raffles were held by the four major charities.

   _____

   _____

   _____

3. A few problems were encountered by the test crew.

   _____

   _____

   _____

4. Even though they tasted of tin, the peas were eaten by the sullen inmates.

_____

_____

_____

5. Although we were soaked to the skin, we were led on toward Denton Lake by our backwoods guide.

_____

_____

_____

5c Varying Sentence Types

Almost everyone feels the monotony when one sentence type is repeated over and over again. To experience such monotony, read the following sentences aloud.

> Reasonably priced apartments are hard to find. Large security deposits are required to move in. Legally binding leases are difficult to negotiate. Pet owners are not allowed to rent.

Monotony occurs when subjects, verbs, objects, and articles all fall in the same places, in the same order, in the same cadence.

Here are three techniques for creating pleasant variation in prose rhythms.

First, mix sentence types. In the following examples, a simple sentence is followed by a compound or complex sentence. (If you wish to review the definitions of sentence types, please see Chapter 7.)

> A Southwest tarantula nestled comfortably among the crated cantaloupes. (Simple sentence) The hand-sized spider was virtually harmless, but grocery shoppers in Peoria fled the store in horror. (Compound sentence)

> A Southwest tarantula nestled comfortably among the crated cantaloupes. (Simple sentence) Although the hand-sized spider was virtually harmless, grocery shoppers in Peoria fled the store in horror. (Complex sentence)

Exercise 5.6 | Write two sentences of different types on the topic, Fads.

_____

_____

_____

_____

Second, vary long and short sentences.

By carefully timing "technological breakthroughs," some stereo manufacturers resell to the same customers every two or three years. (Long sentence) "New" means "necessary" to the audiophile. (Short sentence)

Exercise 5.7 | Write a long and a short sentence on the topic, Exercise.

_____

_____

_____

_____

Third, vary sentence beginnings.

(Subject beginning) A sailboat requires regular maintenance. (Dependent-clause beginning) Whether docked in a slip or stored on a trailer, the boat needs a coat of leaded paint below the waterline every eighteen months. (Prepositional-phrase beginning) Above the water, dozens of cleats, turnbuckles, and winches wait to be cleaned and oiled. (Back to subject beginning again) A sailor's work pays for a sailor's pleasure.

(See Chapter 7 if you wish to review the parts of the sentence.)

Exercise 5.8 | Write three sentences, each with a different form of beginning, on the topic, Magazines.

1. _____
   _____

2. _____
   _____

3. _____
   _____

5d Emphasizing Important Words Through Placement

5d(1) Valuing the Strong Slots

Readers pay particular attention to the *first* and *last* parts of every sentence. Important sentence information usually falls in these positions.

> <u>Nylon strings</u> for classical guitar have almost entirely <u>supplanted gut strings.</u>

As we read this sentence, we concentrate on the beginning few words in an effort to determine the actor, or subject. We then hurry along to the end of the sentence to discover new information about the actor. These positions of special concentration are the sentence's *strong slots.* They give the writer an opportunity to put significant words where they are sure to strike the reader in an emphatic way.*

Exercise 5.9 In the following five sentences, the initial strong slot has been wasted by filling it with nondescript, unimportant words. Rewrite each sentence so that significant words (usually actors) fall in the initial strong-slot position.

1. <u>It is because</u> Ralph arrived late that Sally missed her train.

   _____

2. <u>By not buying</u> unleaded gas, Martin saved $16 per month.

   _____

*Sometimes, you may choose to sacrifice the emphasis of using the strong slot for the sake of sentence variety or special effect.

3. <u>While trying to enjoy</u> the Crushed Rock Symphony, Max played with his Rubik's cube.

_____

4. <u>There is one way</u> that I know of to determine the gold content of a ring.

_____

5. <u>Unless it is possible</u> for him to find a suitable business partner, he will forfeit his interest in the property.

_____

Exercise 5.10 The final strong slot can also be wasted if the writer fills it with insignificant words. Repair the following sentences.

1. His tape deck was never returned, <u>however</u>.

_____

_____

_____

2. Dr. Benson reminded me of my favorite uncle <u>in some ways</u>.

_____

_____

_____

3. The captain steered a course between the coral reefs, <u>nevertheless</u>.

_____

_____

_____

4. Male tortoises have an indentation on their undershells, <u>for example</u>.

_____

_____

_____

5. All the elevators on the Eiffel Tower were shut down for repair,
   <u>unfortunately.</u>

   _____

   _____

   _____

While these sentences cannot be faulted on strict grammatical grounds,
they do create a feeling of anticlimax by wasting the final strong slot.

Exercise 5.11 | Create sentences that emphasize both of the words assigned below. Use
one in the initial strong slot, the other in the final strong slot.

HARVEST; STARVATION: _____

_____

COIN; FOUNTAIN: _____

_____

PALM-READER; FATE: _____

_____

EGGS; NUTRITION: _____

_____

5d(2) Placing the Subject First

Consider the process by which readers make sense out of your writing: pro-
ceeding word by word, left to right, your readers accumulate meanings in
an effort to grasp your whole statement. The *subject* of the sentence provides the first major clue for such meaning-making.

Notice how uncomfortable we are with the delayed subject:

By reputation a dreary and punitive experience, but this time proving to
be educational and even mildly enjoyable, Traffic School came to an end.

By contrast, we appreciate knowing the subject early in the sentence.

> Traffic School, by reputation a dreary and punitive experience, finally came to an end; in all, it proved to be educational and even mildly enjoyable.

Exercise 5.12 In each of the misbegotten sentences below, the subject has been delayed too long. Restore it to an earlier position by rewriting each sentence.

1. Making chemistry his sole activity and participating in no extra-curricular activities, Rod missed the fun of college.

   _____

   _____

   _____

2. Adding spice to their sauces and providing color as well, cayenne is used freely by Mexican cooks.

   _____

   _____

   _____

3. Barking up the wrong tree and defending an enormous territory not his own, the neighborhood was terrorized by Spot.

   _____

   _____

   _____

4. Asking what skills and cash the prospective immigrant brought with him, the New Zealand visa official filled out a long form.

   _____

   _____

   _____

5. Paging through the classified ads and making large circles here and there, apartment hunting was begun by Patty.

_____

_____

_____

5d(3)   Placing the Verb Close to the Subject

Just as the subject (Who?) can be delayed too long, so the verb (. . . did what?) can be postponed with poor results.

> Frank, sensing his unwitting involvement in the destruction of important evidence, perspired. (Verb delayed)

As a general rule, readers of English like to have their basic question, "Who did what?", satisfied as soon as possible. Subjects and their verbs, therefore, should hang together as tightly as possible in most of your sentences. Sometimes, of course, the demands of sentence variety, rhythm, or emphasis will override this general rule. As a matter of usual course, however, give your reader both the subject and its verb, and then add whatever else you wish.

Exercise 5.13   Restore the verb to an earlier position in each of the following sentences.

1. Volcanoes, releasing internal pressures built up over hundreds of years, erupt violently.

_____

_____

_____

2. Winter grasses, lacking necessary moisture as the hot, dry summer comes on, wither.

_____

_____

_____

3. Saddle shoes, though once the end-all and be-all of social sophistication on campus, were out.

_____

_____

_____

4. A conservatory vocalist, Adam, in order to sing just below pitch for an entire punk concert, had to be retrained.

_____

_____

_____

5. Her destiny, full of danger yet also full of ecstasy and fulfillment, waited.

_____

_____

_____

5d(4) Avoiding the *And* Beginning

Use caution in beginning a sentence with *and* in formal essay prose. Too often, *and* prefaces an afterthought that should have been joined more tightly to the foregoing sentence.

NOT: Counterfeiters concentrated their efforts on $100 bills. *And* then merchants "got wise," refusing to cash such large bills without identification.

INSTEAD: Counterfeiters concentrated their efforts on $100 bills. But merchants soon "got wise," refusing to cash such large bills without identification.

Exercise 5.14 Rewrite the following sentence, removing *and* from the initial strong slot.

Ms. Murlins inherited the position from her father, Horatio. And she, no doubt, will pass the job along to her child.

_____

_____

_____

5e Being Specific

5e(1) Identifying *This*

Do not use *this* alone to refer back to an idea or set of facts. A writer who uses the vague *this* risks a breakdown in communication. Readers often cannot, or will not, insert the correct referent for the vague *this* but read on nevertheless. Meaning suffers.

> The democratization of the citizenry, together with the unionization of the workers, brought the era of totalitarian government to a halt. This was greeted with joy in the West.

Here we wonder, "This what? This democratization? This unionization? This halting of totalitarian government?"

Writers can solve the *this* problem by placing an identifying word or phrase after *this*. In the case above, we might clarify by adding "This political development was greeted with joy in the West."

Exercise 5.15 Insert an identifying word or two after the vague *this* in each of the following sentences.

1. The bank president insisted that the carpet be green. This

   _____ infuriated Marc, the interior decorator.

2. "Idleness breeds reptiles of the mind." This _____ sug-

   gests that busy hands are happy hands.

3. Building codes require solid rather than hollow doors at all ex-

   terior entrances and exits. This _____ is intended to aid

   in the prevention of fire.

4. Depression brought on subsidiary ills: anxiety, sleeplessness, lack of appetite, and general malaise. This _____ could have been prevented by proper and timely treatment.

5. Without the ingredient titanium, white paint does not cover properly. This _____ caused an industry crisis during the titanium shortage of 1976.

5e(2)   Omitting *It Is* and *There Is/Are* Whenever Possible

Try to define the underlined words in this sentence:

> It is common knowledge among the students that there is a group of bike thieves preying upon the campus.
>
> It = _____ , there = _____ .

Perhaps you had to leave the spaces blank. *It,* in this context, has no meaning by itself and refers back to no earlier referent. Similarly, *there* does not refer to a particular place (as in "right there"). Both *it is* and *there is* are almost meaningless phrases—noises, really, like clearing the throat before speaking. Whenever possible, banish meaningless phrases from your writing.

When you remove *it is* you discover the true subject of your sentence and allow those significant words to fill the initial strong slot.

> ~~It is~~ common knowledge among the students . . .
>
> All the students know . . .

Similarly, when you remove *there is,* you gain the stylistic advantage of an action verb.

> ~~There is~~ a group of bike thieves preying upon the campus . . .
>
> A group of bike thieves preys upon the campus . . .

In short, you have produced a tight, efficient sentence.

> All the students know that a group of bike thieves preys upon the campus.

This revised sentence makes better use of both the strong slots and the actor-action pattern so essential to strong prose.

Exercise 5.16 Revise the following sentences, omitting *it is* and *there is/are.** Convert verbs to the active form wherever possible.

1. It is the sun that attracts winter visitors to Arizona.

   _____

   _____

   _____

2. There is a path that can be found by us through this wilderness.

   _____

   _____

   _____

3. It is the moon that exerts a powerful influence on our tides.

   _____

   _____

   _____

4. There is still some mystery surrounding the nature and origin of Saturn's rings.

   _____

   _____

   _____

5. It is smog that the face of the old statue was eaten away by.

   _____

   _____

   _____

Read your revised versions aloud. Your ear will tell you what a vast improvement you have made by restoring the initial strong slot to its "rightful owner," and converting an *-ing* verb to an action verb.

**Note:* Certainly we are not out to exterminate *it is* and *there is/are* entirely; sometimes the phrases prove useful and even indispensable ("It is morning in Paris by now.").

5f   Eliminating Wordiness

5f(1)   Cutting Out Deadwood

Each word in good prose *matters*. When the word or phrase doesn't matter, prune it away as you would deadwood out of a living tree.

> *Common Forms of Deadwood*
> Unnecessary restatement of an already clear idea
> An unnecessary aside (often beginning with "which, by the way . . .")
> An overextended example

Exercise 5.17   Locate and cross out the deadwood in the following paragraph.

Jenkins came to his first position fresh from college. He had not had another job between the time he graduated and this, his first job. As a computer-science major, he expected a salary in excess of $25,000 per year (which, by the way, was as much as his professors earned with twice the education). His concern for a large salary led him into trouble. For example, he accepted a job 35 miles from home even though his car needed major repairs. The transmission rasped and clicked, the master cylinder leaked like a sieve, and one headlight kept shorting out. Really, to tell the truth, the car was a wreck. Jenkins had to learn the hard way that salary and satisfaction were not synonymous.

5f(2)   Eliminating the Unnecessary *Which* or *That*

Many readers subconsciously tense when they come upon *which* or *that*, especially in the midst of a long sentence. These words often indicate that a new string of meaning, perhaps a long one, must be linked by the reader to what has gone before.

> Gathering her bags about her like a fortress, Marla stared for long moments through the thickening fog at the train, <u>which</u> pulled slowly out of Victoria Station.

Notice the subtle resistance you may feel when, after twenty words, the writer seems to be off on a new start with *which*.

By omitting *which* and *that* whenever possible, the writer tends to make "meaning packages" more compact.

> Gathering her bags about her like a fortress, Marla stared for long moments through the thickening fog at the train pulling slowly out of Victoria Station.

Exercise 5.18 | Rewrite the following sentences to omit *which* or *that*.

1. The Ford Foundation searched for the project that offered the best hope to chronic alcoholics.

   _____

   _____

   _____

2. A bluff that is called Open Hand serves three Indian tribes as a holy place.

   _____

   _____

   _____

3. No one attended the chamber concert, which is why the Culture Committee canceled the rest of the series.

   _____

   _____

   _____

5g Creating Parallels

When enumerating actions, use the same grammatical form for each verb in the series. By creating such grammatical parallels, you help your reader hold several things in mind at once. Remembering grammatically similar actions is easier than remembering dissimilar actions.

NOT: Bob rakes the leaves, is planting flowers, and there are hedges that he trims.

INSTEAD: Bob <u>rakes</u> leaves, <u>plants</u> flowers, and <u>trims</u> hedges.

Exercise 5.19 | Write a sentence in which you enumerate each of the following actions. Make sure that you follow parallel grammatical form.

Mary Ann's duties at Cessna:

Rivet tail section
Responsible for assembling rear rudder
The completion of final wiring

_____

_____

_____

5h Choosing Pronouns

5h(1) Deciding on *I*, *You*, and *We*

The proper use of *I, you,* and *we* depends more on the exercise of judgment than on the application of rigid rules. Certainly these pronouns do occur in fine essays. When *I, you,* and *we* are avoided at all costs, in fact, strange circumlocutions result ("It is the opinion of this writer. . . .").

But when *I* peppers every paragraph, the writer's ego looms too large over the subject at hand. Similarly, the repeated use of *you* in formal essay writing can make your readers feel singled out, bullied, or put upon.

NOT: You know, or should know, from my previous chapter that. . .

A good rule is to use *I* when the only alternative is awkward wordiness. Use *you* even more sparingly. Most of the time *we* (which includes both author and reader) works better than either *I* or *you.*

NOT: I have shown you how vitamin C eradicated certain diseases aboard ship.
INSTEAD: We have seen how vitamin C eradicated certain diseases aboard ship.

Exercise 5.20 | Convert *I* and *my* to *we* and *our* in the following sentence.

I ordinarily assess such actions, in my evaluations of political figures, as mania for power.

_____

_____

_____

_____

Convert *you* and *your* to *we* and *our* in the following sentence.

You seldom believe a person who claims to know your personal destiny.

_____

_____

_____

_____

5h(2) Avoiding the Undefined *One*

In an effort to avoid an undue reliance on *I* and *you,* some writers virtually canonize the personal *one* in their essays. The result is often unnatural, stiff, and impersonal.

NOT: One would think, if one were so inclined, that one's own luxuries might be sacrificed so that one's friends might have necessities.

INSTEAD: We should be willing to sacrifice our luxuries for the sake of our friends' necessities.

Whenever the reader begins to think of *one* as a mysterious personal presence in an essay, the writer has erred. Use *one* sparingly. Consider the following alternatives:

1. Recast in the plural form, substituting *we.*

NOT: One may feel a sense of outrage...

INSTEAD: We may feel a sense of outrage...

2. Substitute *I,* if you intend to talk about yourself.

NOT: One's thesis might be stated as follows...

INSTEAD: I argue that...

3. Recast the sentence to avoid any personal reference.

NOT: One's home town always reminds one of rueful pains and magical pleasures.

INSTEAD: Home towns always recall rueful pains and magical pleasures.

Exercise 5.21 | Rewrite the following sentences to remove *one* effectively.

1. One's choice of wallpaper reveals much about one's personality.

_____

_____

_____

2. What might be effective therapy for one could prove harmful to another.

_____

_____

_____

3. If one chooses, one can reserve the sauna for relaxation after one's exercise.

_____

_____

_____

5i Controlling Paragraph Length

Blocks of print exceeding a half-page in length can discourage a reader. Such paragraphs seem to contain so much to plough through, so much to hold in mind. Test your own feelings. Which of the "pages" below would you prefer to read?

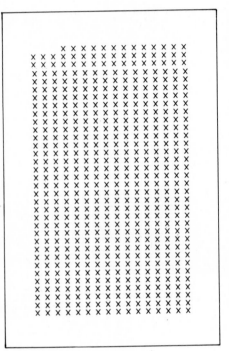 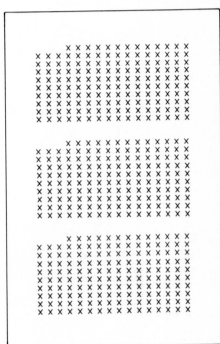

A series of short paragraphs can also pose obstacles to reading. The reader faces the task of organizing large blocks of meaning out of small bits and pieces of prose. Turn to page 82. Do you feel the difficulty of tying together so many discrete packages of information presented on the "page"?

Although short paragraphs can create special impact, their use in essay prose—especially in college papers—should be weighed against one reality: many academic readers view *any* one- or two-sentence paragraph as an undeveloped paragraph. These readers may often be incorrect, but writers must still consider such biases in deciding how best to persuade an academic or professional audience.

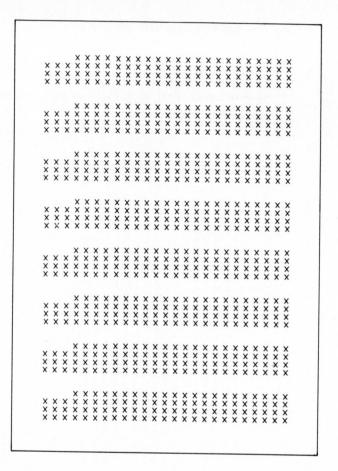

Exercise 5.22 | Rewrite the following short paragraphs as one long paragraph. You may find it necessary to rearrange the short paragraphs.

A foreign ambassador's child was denied entry to California schools because neither of the child's parents was a citizen.

Americans need to reexamine laws governing who may and who may not be admitted to public schools.

Illegal aliens, by contrast, may send their children to public schools, according to a recent California Supreme Court decision.

The foreign ambassador faces an absurd dilemma: his child may not attend school so long as the family's presence in this country is legal but may attend school should their presence ever become illegal.

The question came to a head in California public schools.

5i Avoiding Trite and Slang Expressions

5i(1) Eliminating Trite Expressions

Words and phrases lose their expressive energy when they are always associated with the same context.

Context	Stale, Trite Word
Sharp as a	tack
Straight as an	arrow
Snug as a	bug
Sweet as	honey

Such *cliches* are dead for expressive purposes, and should be avoided.

Words and phrases also may become trite when unnecessary words take the place of simple, direct alternatives.

Unnecessary Words	Direct Alternative
To be in agreement with	agree
To give assistance to	assist, help
To have a preference for	prefer
To be desirous of	want
Due to the fact that	because
Subsequent to	after
At this point in time	now

Finally, some words are trite simply because they don't work well. The prime examples are *very* and *really* (a slang variation of *very*). Consider the sentence, "The toddler sobbed." The insertion of *very* or *really*—"The toddler really sobbed" or "sobbed very much"—does not add to your reader's vision of the sobbing tot. If you intend a more dramatic effect, then add more dramatic words: "The toddler sobbed, lips quivering and pinched eyes streaming."

The use of *very* and *really* is an attempt to make meaning*less* words do what only meaning*ful* words can do.

Exercise 5.23 | Mark out the trite words and phrases in the sentences below. Write in an appropriate substitution.

1. The network finally gave the nod to Beston for the anchor spot on the six o'clock news.

2. Handsome as a prince, Beston stood head and shoulders above the three other candidates.

3. At an earlier time prior to his selection, Beston gave assistance in the production of the news at WKKR in Philadelphia.

4. In the event of Beston's favorable reception by TV viewers, the network has indicated its plans to make an addition to the six o'clock news in the form of a second newscaster.

5j(2) Eliminating Slang Expressions

For the purposes of essay prose, in the contexts shown below the italicized words and phrases should be considered too informal for use:

> She *goes,* "Well, yes, I think so."
> The museum was *kind of/sort of* interesting.
> *Lots/a whole lot of* birds fluttered by.
> I *could of* (for "could have") mastered Kung Fu with practice.
> The waiter brought *way* more than we could eat.
> I wanted to go, *only* (for "but") my parents wouldn't let me.
> The concert was a *real turn-on.*
> The force of sound coming from the huge speakers was *out-rageous.*

You probably noticed that some of the slang words above are already dated. *Outrageous,* for example, and *turn-on* are slang terms of the 70s more than the 80s. Because slang words die so quickly and differ so widely according to region, they are poor communicators for your purposes in essay prose.

Exercise 5.24 Rewrite the following sentences to avoid slang.

1. My grades almost qualified me for medical school, but calculus brought me down.

_____

_____

_____

2. I had seen beautiful sunsets before, but this one was outrageous.

   _____

   _____

   _____

3. Of the forty students standing arm-in-arm in the protest line, only two were eventually busted.

   _____

   _____

   _____

4. Summer jobs overseas can be something else.

   _____

   _____

   _____

No lover of the English language hates slang. Rather than being too simple for essay prose, slang is in fact too complex: it signals all kinds of assumptions about the background and mood of our audience, about the writer's bond with the reader, and about the writer's emotional and social responses to the content of the essay. The use of slang often suggests that the writer knows the reader intimately. When such is not the case, the use of slang may be ineffective at best and offensive at worst.

5k Avoiding a Posed and Overwritten Style

To avoid rhetorical posing, prune away portions of your writing that call attention, in a self-conscious or showy way, to the essay itself, to the act of writing the essay, or to your own feelings.*

NOT: Before I conclude this paper, let me insert a few lines regarding . . .

---

*Certainly your own feelings play a vital role in your writing. The error of "showcasing" emotions occurs when the writer places an undue or inappropriate emphasis on his or her feelings.

NOT: When I first considered writing this paper, I drew to mind several possible topics.

NOT: Never, never, I tell you, have I felt such loathing, and that's from the bottom of my heart.

Exercise 5.25 | Rewrite the following sentence to remove rhetorical posing.

Before going on to the next paragraph, I ask each of my readers to call to mind moments of fright from childhood.

_____

_____

_____

5l Avoiding Contractions and Abbreviations

5l(1) Avoiding Contractions

Gradually some contractions, such as *let's, we've, isn't, aren't,* and a few others, are gaining acceptance in essay prose. The following contractions, however, should not be used in formal writing:

> she'll (he'll)
> they'll
> you'll
> could've
> should've
> they've
> don't
> doesn't

Again, academic readers continue to have strong attitudes toward the place of contractions in formal prose. Before writing an important paper, you should know your professor's preference regarding the use of contractions. Many teachers still insist on seeing no contractions at all in term paper prose.

Exercise 5.26 | Rewrite the following sentences, converting the contractions to more formal alternatives.

1. The idea could've worked, but necessary financing wasn't available.

   _____

   _____

   _____

2. While unmanned space travel would've been less difficult than a manned space program, purely mechanical ships couldn't have caught the public imagination as powerfully as an astronaut speaking from space.

   _____

   _____

   _____

5l(2) Avoiding Abbreviations

A few terms are known primarily in their abbreviated form, such as AFL-CIO, LSD, and NATO. Forms of address, titles, and degrees are also abbreviated in formal prose: Ms., Mr., Mrs., Dr., Rev., Ph.D., M.A., B.A. Almost all other words are better spelled out in formal writing.

In college and career writing, the most abused abbreviation is *etc.* Often, in enumerating the qualities of an object or experience, we know that we haven't listed *all* of the items possible.

NOT: The restored MG was a flash of color, chrome and leather, etc.

We know, of course, that the car also contained aluminum, glass, plastic, and a host of other materials. We do not have to append *etc.* to our list as a way of indicating the existence of these other items. Our readers assume that our list of three items is merely suggestive, not exhaustive.

When you are faced with enumerating many items, consider selecting three major items to represent all the rest. Do not append *etc.* to the list. You may want to conclude with an identifying phrase.

He sprinkled in marjoram, thyme, mint, *and other spices.*

Exercise 5.27 | Rewrite the following sentences, replacing the abbreviations.

1. The am't. of air pollutants in the atmosphere today is less per capita than during the eighteenth cent.

   _____

   _____

   _____

2. Students from N.Y.C. had trouble adapting to the slower pace in the mountains N. of L.A.

   _____

   _____

   _____

Complete the following sentences by listing at least three items. Do not use *etc.*

1. From the airplane I could see _____

   _____

   _____

2. The disc jockey mixed several musical styles: _____

   _____

   _____

3. Lining the shelves were _____

   _____

   _____

5m   Using Parentheses Correctly

Parentheses mark off an occasional explanatory or incidental comment.

Agoraphobia (fear of open spaces) plagues thousands of businesspeople forced by their jobs to travel.

Parentheses should not be used to insert afterthoughts or coy remarks into formal writing. When the "voice" speaking within the parentheses is clever and diverting, the voice speaking outside the parentheses may seem dry and lifeless. The reader begins to discount the importance of one voice, favoring the other.

Speak in one voice to your reader, not two.

NOT: Japanese koi fish can cost hundreds of dollars (unless, of course, your Uncle Harry raises them as mine does.)

INSTEAD: Japanese koi fish can cost hundreds of dollars. But because my Uncle Harry raises them, . . .

Exercise 5.28 | Rewrite the following sentences to remove misused parentheses.

1. Simon and Garfunkel (who, by the way, I still like after all these years) restored the art of poetry to song lyrics.

    _____

    _____

    _____

2. The word *ninny* (didn't you ever call your brother or sister a ninny?) comes from the word, *innocent.*

    _____

    _____

    _____

3. Catalina Island (I heard it was once the private estate of the Wrigley family) has now been deeded to the state of California.

    _____

    _____

    _____

4. The old silver spoon (Mother thought it was the same one that fed her grandfather) lay neglected at the bottom of the drawer.

    _____

    _____

    _____

5n   Avoiding Unnecessary Questions

No reader enjoys being "set up" by an artificial and unnecessary question.

The senator rose from his chair and arranged his notes. <u>Was he about to begin a filibuster?</u> Yes. The rest of the senate sank back in resignation.

Writers turn to such questions in an effort to bring suspense to their prose. The attempt almost never fails. When writers hang the carrot of an artificial question before the reader, they breed impatience and even hostility. "If you know the answer," the reader grumbles, "why ask the question? Simply get *on* with it!"

Proper questions, by contrast, are questions for which the writer, too, seeks an answer.

The mathematics of space travel raises an interesting question: Can we ever expect to propel a physical object fast enough to reach the nearest star within the span of a human life?

Exercise 5.29 | Rewrite the following sentences to remove artificial questions.

1. Frank rose early to ride to work on the M.T.A. But did he ever return? No, he never returned.

   _____

   _____

   _____

2. Ralph's parents gave him twenty-one years of caring and love. But did he show a bit of concern for them in their later years? No. He selfishly pursued his own interests.

   _____

   _____

   _____

3. Materialism is often said to be not so much the curse as the inheritance of the present generation. Are we fated to perpetual slavery to the dollar? I don't think so.

_____

_____

_____

5o Choosing Words Carefully

Use long, uncommon words in your writing *only* when they add significant meaning that can't be rendered in simpler ways. Never use "twenty-five cent" words merely to impress your reader.

NOT: Benson's argumentation was less than persuasive to the rational powers of the majority of the populace.

INSTEAD: Benson's argument failed to win over most thinking people.

Exercise 5.30 | Restore clear, direct English to the following sentences. Use your dictionary as necessary.

1. Her animadversions notwithstanding, Lady Carolyn transferred the obsequious courtier to her sister's retinue.

   _____

   _____

   _____

2. Bill expounded an initial perception about the mechanism by which the security alarm operated.

   _____

   _____

   _____

3. Sarah queried her sibling, Dian, regarding the emotive realities extant subsequent to Dale's departure.

   _____

   _____

5p   Avoiding Awkward Constructions and Repetitions

5p(1)   Avoiding Awkward Constructions

Sometimes writers join words together in ways that are grammatically correct, but stylistically wrong. The awkward passages feel odd; they look strange and sound awry.

Here are a few of the more common causes of awkwardness:

1. Unintentional rhymes.

   NOT: The nightlife in <u>Paris</u> might <u>embarrass</u> the <u>heiress</u>.

2. Similar consecutive word endings.

   NOT: We attended the <u>nation</u>'s <u>coronation</u> <u>celebration</u>.

3. Anticlimactic use of the final strong slot.

   NOT: Even though I was sweltering, 98 degrees was all that <u>it was up to</u>.

4. Overextended passages of alliteration (the same beginning consonant in successive words).

   NOT: Burly brown clouds burst into view, boiling above the bent banyan boughs.

5. One word construction forced into service for another, more natural, construction.

   NOT: Barbara didn't understand Frank <u>being angry</u>.

Exercise 5.31 | Rewrite each of the following sentences to avoid awkward phrases.

1. Shirley found it easy to repair the bicycle from being mechanical.

   _____

   _____

   _____

2. Alliance Farm Equipment was able to build twelve hoes a day in Bodega Bay.

    _____

    _____

    _____

3. Poirot finally determined who mailed the letter and whom the letter was to.

    _____

    _____

    _____

4. One factor brought chaos to the delegation: election dissension.

    _____

    _____

    _____

5. Tapered trousers tend to attract teen-age tap dancers.

    _____

    _____

    _____

5p(2)   Avoiding Repetitions

Often, simple words or phrases are repeated unnecessarily, with an awkward result. Usually these repetitions occur in two places:

1. The last word of one sentence is repeated to begin the next sentence.

    NOT: Her favorite color was *crimson. Crimson* made her feel alive and rather royal.

    Solution: Find an alternate word or phrase for the repeated word. Words with similar meanings are *synonyms.*

    Her favorite color was crimson. The ruddy shade made her feel alive and rather royal.

2. The same word is repeated in the initial strong slots of succeeding sentences.

NOT: <u>Gravity</u>, though experienced by all, remains a mystery. <u>Gravity</u> currently occupies the efforts of theoretical physicists at Cambridge University. <u>Gravity</u>, so far, has defied attempts to construct a specific model demonstrating its nature and physical operations.

Solution: Choose sentence beginnings that do not include the repeated word.

Gravity, though experienced by all, remains a mystery. Theoretical physicists at Cambridge University currently are studying this natural force...

Exercise 5.32 | Revise the following sentences so that unfortunate repetitions do not occur.

1. Professional soccer in the United States has talent, but lacks money. Money has been the root cause of the controversies to wrack the sport.

   _____

   _____

   _____

2. A door-to-door salesperson inevitably develops an unassailable self-image. Self-image is the salesperson's only shield against countless slammed doors.

   _____

   _____

   _____

3. No one in Frank's family had attended college. College meant needless hours away from the farm.

   _____

   _____

   _____

Recap

We have discussed fifteen matters of style and practiced applying them.

1. 5b   Using the active voice
2. 5c   Varying sentence types
3. 5d   Emphasizing important words through placement
4. 5e   Being specific
5. 5f   Eliminating wordiness
6. 5g   Creating parallels
7. 5h   Choosing pronouns
8. 5i   Controlling paragraph length
9. 5j   Avoiding trite and slang expressions
10. 5k   Avoiding a posed and overwritten style
11. 5l   Avoiding contractions and abbreviations
12. 5m   Using parentheses correctly
13. 5n   Avoiding unnecessary questions
14. 5o   Choosing words carefully
15. 5p   Avoiding awkward constructions and repetitions

Review Test: Writing with Style

Chapter 5 began with a paragraph exemplifying what *not* to do in terms of style. Notice that each of the stylistic errors above are identified by number in that paragraph, which is reprinted below for convenience. Rewrite the paragraph, removing or repairing all stylistic errors. Feel free to add words or sentences as necessary. You may decide to break the paragraph into two or more paragraphs.

Police Chief and Daily Times *Feud Over Dageford Case*

[1] Yesterday the decision that was made by the police chief was to defend his officers against all charges in the Dageford case. [2] The response that was made by the *Daily Times* was to challenge the chief to make all files public on the matter. [3] And as a result [4] this caused [5] irritation on the part of the chief. Here are the facts. Two officers arrested Dageford, editor of the *Daily Times,* for running a red light on June 14.

They [6] read him his rights, were securing him to the steering wheel with handcuffs, and then the alleged verbal berating of the arrested man began. [7] One would think that you could use less force in such an arrest. [8] They were [9] laying it on rather thick. [10] Let us underline the point that Dageford [11] didn't show any am't. of resistance [12] (the officers said he struggled violently). [13] What happened next? Dageford's [14] involuntary detention in full public view was prolonged for more than an hour while the officers questioned him. [15] The officers questioned him, Dageford claims, to embarrass the *Daily Times.* The officers and the chief have no comment on Dageford's charges.

Writing Topics: Practicing Style

Practice applying the stylistic matters discussed in this chapter by writing paragraphs developed from the following topics.

Assertive Topics

1. Cities should/should not be allowed to limit population growth.
2. Zoos are/are not humane environments for wild animals.
3. Nations should/should not own territories beyond their national boundaries.
4. Home bomb shelters are/are not a necessary part of modern civil defense.
5. The military draft is/is not necessary for national security.

Descriptive Topics

1. Describe the atmosphere at your favorite restaurant.
2. Describe an especially comfortable (or uncomfortable) spot on your college campus.
3. Describe the most unusual hair style you have seen.
4. Describe the ways in which some public place—a college building, a bus stop, a grocery store—shows wear and tear.
5. Describe the face of the President of the United States.

Narrative Topics

1. Narrate a few of the events leading to a recent political success or failure.
2. Narrate the recent actions of a popular musician or musical group.
3. Narrate the activity at your home ten minutes before important company arrives.
4. Narrate a few of the events following a difficult decision in your life.
5. Narrate the actions of an organization you respect for its humanitarianism.

Chapter 6
Writing the Essay

Rod, twenty, describes his severe writing problems to you. After considering his dilemma, try to explain to him what seems to be going wrong. Then offer any helpful suggestions that occur to you.

ROD: I'm on probation at this university for only one reason: I can't write. I had a *B* in European History up until the term paper. I got a *D*– on the paper and a *C*– in the course. Research isn't the problem. I have stacks of index cards filled with all kinds of information. I just freeze up when I try to write. The only way I am able to get anything down on the page at all is to wait until the night before the paper is due. Then my adrenalin level is so high from panic that I just put anything down, helter-skelter. I can't figure it out. I always got *A*s on grammar and spelling tests. I can diagram sentences just fine. If I do try to begin a paper long before the deadline, I just sit there putting down a sentence, crossing it out, trying another, then crossing it out. Believe me, I really do try to write, but what comes out—if anything—sounds stupid to me. I'll admit that I've been buying my papers lately. But at $5 a page, I can't afford that very long. I just can't figure it out.

Offer a possible explanation for Rod's problem with writing.

_____

_____

_____

_____

Now offer one or two helpful suggestions.

_____

_____

_____

_____

Your skill in writing an essay will help you master several major writing forms:

Term papers
College or business reports
Scientific papers
Formal letters
Book, art, and theatre reviews
Personal or career-goal compositions, often required for job or school applications

In this chapter, we will practice a four-step "recipe" of sorts for essay composition. The steps are (1) *mental preparation*, (2) *architecture*, (3) *rough draft*, (4) *polished draft*. With practice, these steps can drastically reduce the time, effort, and agony spent in writer's block, false starts, word searches, and discarded essays. At first the steps may seem mechanical. Quickly, though, they can become natural habits—*good* habits that come to the rescue, especially when time is short and the pressure is on.

6a Mental Preparation

MARGARET: I used to try to write while watching "M.A.S.H." and doing my nails. It took me hours to write a single page. I would get a good idea, start putting it down, and then I'd be interrupted by something—the TV show, a funny spot on my fingernail, maybe a peanut-butter sandwich. Then I couldn't get on track again. Nothing seemed to hang together.

The first step in mental preparation is to *clear the decks.* Good writing involves concentration. When beginning to write, give yourself a period of time uncommitted to other activities.

Next, attack the essay as a challenge; be confident. An essay of several hundred words, like a long walk, always looks wearisome at first. But take the first steps and soon the pleasure of making progress overcomes feelings of disappointment.

Finally, *avoid the panic of deadlines.* All sorts of poor compromises are made in a frenzied effort to meet deadlines. Plan ahead.

6a(1) Know Yourself

MARGARET: I went through different voices. First I sounded like *World Book* encyclopedia when I wrote. Then, in an effort to seem more sophisticated, I mimicked insurance contracts, with lots of *therebys, whomevers,* and *heretofores.* I finally got sick of playing ventriloquist. I took the big risk: I wrote a paper that sounded like *me.* I think I got a *B* on that paper. What I do remember clearly is the absolute sense of relief I felt. I didn't have to fake it anymore. Papers written in my own voice were OK. They were definitely easier to write. I had never been an insurance-contract lawyer.

When others read what you write, they hear a voice and a personality—*yours.* Some beginning writers make an effort to hide or distort that voice. They dislike the way they sound when they write. By using unfamiliar words and sentence forms, such writers try to hide behind a mask of language.

Use the following exercise to help yourself "hear" your own natural mode of expression. Get to know and like those native habits. If you want your natural voice to grow and mature, use it freely.

Exercise 6.1 Rewrite the following sentences in a style that seems natural and comfortable to you.

1. At a time prior to the interactive mixing of Cubans and U.S. citizens in the region of Miami, Florida, the general attitudes of the populace regarding bilingualism in those schools available to the public were primarily negative.

_____

_____

_____

_____

2. We saw an otter. We were rafting down the Eel River. The otter swam alongside the raft. He hissed at us. He tried to chase us from his territory.

_____

_____

_____

_____

_____

3. Ridding herself of her parachute, the young woman—twenty, twenty-one, no more—dove repeatedly beneath the battering waves as the aircraft sank, nose first, into the frothy sea.

_____

_____

_____

_____

_____

Now review the passages you have written. For better or for worse, you have taken the most important step toward writing success: you have preferred *your* voice over that of another writer, another personality. The most effective way to become a skilled writer is to build upon, refine, and trust that natural voice.

6a(2) Know Your Audience

MARGARET: I used to feel like Abe Lincoln writing for posterity: "Fourscore and seven years ago, when I began this composition . . ." Posterity frightened me out of my words. It was like standing in front of millions and millions of people.

Now I forget about posterity and ask myself one question: Who will be reading my essay? If, for example, the members of my composition class are my audience, then I choose language and examples that they will find interesting. If my audience is just my geology professor, as on an essay exam, then I try to bend toward what he wants to see in the essay.

This is not a speech on "oh how good I am." But I do find it much easier to write when I can begin to imagine how my audience will understand my words.

Exercise 6.2   Rewrite the following sentence for each of the audiences indicated.

My car has been giving me fits.

1. Audience: your mechanic

_____

_____

_____

2. Audience: a six-year-old child

_____

_____

_____

3. Audience: Uncle Jeff, who gave you the car as a present

_____

_____

_____

4. Audience: a foreign visitor who speaks little English

_____

_____

_____

You and Your Audience

The ease with which we write depends to a great degree on our attitudes toward our readers. As we discussed in Chapter 1, if the audience for our prose is critical and harsh, then the act of writing will be difficult. We will feel threatened at every turn by possible errors, punishable, it sometimes seems, by death or worse! But if we feel that we have the respect and affection of our audience, we relax and our writing blooms with feeling, wit, and even beauty. As we relax, interestingly, we make fewer grammatical errors; we do not force ourselves into strange and stilted constructions.

    The key question is this: how do you come to *know* your readers' attitudes toward your writing? Probably their feelings can be predicted by assessing your own. Imagine, for example, that a classmate must read an essay aloud to your writing class. Your own feelings, as a listener, are neither judgmental nor negative. You find yourself interested in what your classmate has to say. You are tolerant of slips and mistakes here and there. In short, you're friendly and patient.

No doubt your audience has similar attitudes toward your writing. By assuming that your readers are on *your* side, you free yourself to write with ease and grace. You have no need for defensive poses and self-conscious wanderings. You write openly and clearly because you believe your audience to be both sympathetic and interested.

Exercise 6.3 | Revise the following paragraph. Direct it to an audience that likes and respects you. Feel free to add or subtract material from the paragraph.

No one can tell me that tobacco subsidies in this country make any sense at all. The Surgeon General makes a claim that not one of you dares to deny: cigarettes are a health hazard. Then the federal government turns right around and sends millions of dollars to tobacco farmers to support the tobacco industry. You don't have to have much of an I.Q. to determine with me that this practice is senseless. And what do you do about it? Just sit there, because you don't really care who lives or dies, do you?

MARGARET: His name really was Snodgrass. I didn't make it up. He was my writing instructor, and he scared me silly. He had such a bitter way of attacking student papers. He was correct, of course, in what he had to say about our grammar. But his attitude told us loud and clear that he didn't like us, didn't like our ideas, and didn't like having to teach us.

Writing for Mr. Snodgrass was one of the greatest writing challenges I've ever faced. It was impossible to assume that my audience (Mr. S.) liked and respected me. He didn't.

So I assumed the impossible. For my sake, not his, I pretended that he was interested in what I had to say; that he thought I was bright, personable, and sometimes insightful.

Immediately the essays became easier to write. I no longer paralyzed myself with anxieties over Mr. Snodgrass's attitudes.

You probably can guess how it all turned out. There were no *A* papers; Snodgrass didn't turn into a human being; and he didn't write any letters to the scholarship committee on my behalf.

In the end I got a *B −* in the course. I kept my confidence, though. I needed some confidence to write, and he couldn't take it away.

When Your Audience Is a Professor

Many of your college compositions, reports, and essay tests will be read by an audience of one: the professor. Sometimes you may come to know your professor well during the course of the semester. At other times, your audience of one can remain as impersonal and unknown as your mail carrier may be. How does a writer develop a sense of audience when the audience is a professor?

Unless your instructor suggests otherwise, write for your professor as you would for a general audience of interested, literate readers. Even if you have developed a friendship with your professor and know, let's say, of her love for sailing, you should still write to your broader audience. It would not do, for example, to defend ocean ecology in an essay by drawing in your professor's "own delight in sailing clean, blue waters."

Your professor will not always provide a guide and focus for your writing. By asking you to write for a broad, literate audience, your professor is giving you practice in skills that will carry over into your personal and career writing after graduation.

Exercise 6.4 | Each of the following paragraphs refers to a professor's specific interests. Revise the sentences so that they speak to a broad, literate audience. Omit any materials you wish; substitute new material freely.

1. You seem to be the kind of woman who understands the meaning of disappointment in matters of the heart. You'll be sympathetic, then, when I explain in this essay how traumatic it can be to suddenly end a relationship that was supposed to lead to marriage.

   _____

   _____

   _____

   _____

   _____

   _____

2. Rock-collecting brings the excitement of the quest and the satisfaction of discovery. Last summer my father and I trekked through the remote Brown Mountains of Arizona seeking garnets. These purple gems are similar in many ways to the rubies I have noticed and admired on the ring you often wear.

   _____

   _____

   _____

   _____

   _____

   _____

3. When people join together in a professional or trade union, they inevitably sacrifice some of their own attitudes and principles for the "good" of the union. I know that you're a member of the Teachers' Union. You probably would be ostracized if you openly agreed with the position I express in this essay. But if your heart tells you that I am right, please put a "+" in the margin. I'll know what you mean. Trust me not to tell the others.

   _____

   _____

_____

_____

_____

_____

_____

6a(3) Know Your Topic

MARGARET: One time I chose to write a 500-word essay on musical instruments. I was a graduate, after all, of Miss Pruit's Elementary Piano Class for Preschoolers. Later I had tried clarinet in junior high school.

What a disaster my choice was! After 36 words on the piano and 19 on the clarinet, I knew I was in trouble. I just didn't have enough to say about my topic.

I complained to my uncle, who plays double bass in the City Symphony. Secretly, I hoped he would instantly give me about 450 words of good material. Instead, he asked me questions. What instrument did I like best? Why? What are instruments supposed to do for us? Are there any new instruments? His questions went on and on.

To make a long story short, I soon had enough ideas for ten essays. I knew more than I thought I did.

Perhaps half of all writing blocks occur simply because the writer does not know what to say. The well, so to speak, runs dry.

Joe has set out to write a report on the problems of nuclear-waste disposal. At the end of page one he writes:

These examples demonstrate that radioactive materials, no matter how carefully sealed up, eventually contaminate both deep-soil and deep-ocean disposal sites.

Joe had anticipated filling four or five pages on this timely topic. But what does he do now? Certainly he can't begin to summarize after only one page.

Joe finds himself stuck with writer's block because he didn't *know his topic* before he began to write.

Brainstorming

The surest way to have enough to say is to have *more* than enough to say. Toward that end, consider using an invention technique popularized by the classical Greek orators. The technique is called *brainstorming* and involves using a loose structure of questions to stimulate ideas about a topic.

Many writers suffer from the "blank wall" syndrome. They stare at the wall or off into space, hoping that writing ideas will magically appear. To understand just how frustrating the blank-wall approach can be, take a minute or two to consider materials you might use for an essay on one of the following topics:

Reincarnation
Puppy Love
Manual Skills
Rings
Illness

Your minute or two of unstructured reflection may not have produced a wealth of images, ideas, and examples on your topic. Instead, you may have felt the beginnings of discouragement.

Useful Questions for Brainstorming

Using the same topic you chose above, work your way quickly through the twelve brainstorming questions below. In the space provided, jot down in brief form any notions, details, or examples stimulated by the question at hand. (Fill in your topic wherever the blank occurs in the question.)

1. If no one (or everyone) had _____ , how would the world be

   different?

   Jottings

   _____   _____

   _____   _____

   _____   _____

2. What kind of people find _____ especially tempting, inter-

esting, or valuable? Why?

Jottings

_____   _____

_____   _____

_____   _____

3. For certain periods of my life, I was almost unaware (or particularly

aware) of _____ . Why?

Jottings

_____   _____

_____   _____

_____   _____

4. _____ is/are usually associated with a certain part of the

world. Why?

Jottings

_____   _____

_____   _____

_____   _____

5. Few (many) people lie awake at night thinking about _____ .

Why?

Jottings

_____   _____

_____   _____

_____   _____

6. _____ can have an impact on human emotions. How?

Jottings

_____   _____

_____   _____

_____   _____

7. _____ , in spite of its/their surface simplicity, has/have a deeper significance. What is it?

Jottings

_____   _____

_____   _____

_____   _____

8. _____ arouse(s) widely different memories.

For some, _____

For others, _____

For a few, _____

Jottings

_____   _____

_____   _____

_____   _____

9. _____ can be divided into major parts.

First, _____

Second, _____

Third, _____

Jottings

_____   _____

_____   _____

_____   _____

10. _____ might be wholly unnecessary

if _____

if _____

if _____

Jottings

_____   _____

_____   _____

_____   _____

11. _____ is not the way it was in the past.

Formerly, _____

At present, _____

In the future, _____

Jottings

_____   _____

_____   _____

_____   _____

12. When I think of _____ , three images come to mind.

First, _____

Second, _____

Third, _____

Jottings

_____   _____

_____   _____

_____   _____

Your jottings, of course, have not fallen into an exact working outline for an essay. For now, the goal is simply to bring to consciousness as many ideas, images, and examples as possible. At a later stage, you can select and organize your favorite ideas and details for use in an essay.

Exercise 6.5 | Select a topic that interests you. If nothing comes to mind, choose one topic from the list below.

Flight
Dragons
Cheating
Caves
Poverty

Use the twelve brainstorming techniques to generate a wealth of possibilities. Keep a record of your ideas by jotting brief notes in the space provided.

1. _____   _____

   _____   _____

   _____   _____

   _____   _____

2. _____   _____

   _____   _____

   _____   _____

   _____   _____

3. _____   _____

   _____   _____

   _____   _____

   _____   _____

4. _____   _____

   _____   _____

   _____   _____

   _____   _____

5. _____   _____

   _____   _____

   _____   _____

6. _____

7. _____

8. _____

9. _____

10. _____

11. _____

12. _____   _____

    _____   _____

    _____   _____

    _____   _____

For now, let's assume that library research is unnecessary because your essay draws on your own personal experiences and opinions. Appendix C treats the topic of library research, including the use of quotations and footnotes.

6b Architecture

6b(1) Shaping the Topic

Let's assume that successful brainstorming has produced for you a wealth of ideas, facts, images, details, and examples; but they are all scattered in bits and pieces. Now begins the task of *architecture*: shaping selected bits into the essay structure you intend.

Limiting the Topic

Many beginning writers hesitate to limit a topic, particularly one assigned by an instructor. Limited topics, they fear, don't cover enough ground, and may not meet the instructor's expectation.

Usually such assumptions are wrong. Broad essay topics (Life, Patriotism, Goals) invite shallow judgments, superficial examples, and recurring half-truths. Limited topics, by contrast, let the writer bite off only enough to chew. By allowing the writer to deal with a specific area of personal experience, interest, or expertise, limited topics lead to essays that are simply truer.

When you wish to limit a topic assigned in class, discuss your intent with your instructor.

Look back for a moment to the wealth of ideas generated by your brainstorms in the previous exercise. Not all ideas and images can or should be used. By limiting your topic, you determine which set of ideas seems most promising for use in your essay.

Notice in the following jottings how the writer has circled ideas and examples that seem to fit together.

Topic: Psychotherapy

Jottings

Old methods of long term analysis

Manias, obsessions, compulsions

Mental health hospitals

Freud, Jung

Use of hypnotism

Difference between psychiatrist and psychologist

The word *bedlam*

(Eating and anxieties)

Rule of one-thirds: one-third get better, one-third get worse, one-third stay the same

(Success with weight control)

(Commercial weight-control clinics)

Social attitudes toward mental illness

Technical meaning of neurosis, psychosis

Electroshock therapy

(Behavior-modification techniques)

(Dieting failures)

(Weight-watching support groups)

More health plans now pay for mental health care

You may wonder how the writer knew which ideas and details to circle. Often the writer *cannot* decide how to limit the topic until he or she has considered many possibilities. The writer must evaluate the possibilities one by one; some are too large to write about, some too narrow; some ideas seem stimulating, others seem flat. But in the course of such evaluation, a group of related ideas begins to merge and take shape. Out of all the possibilities, the writer limits the topic to a set of related ideas, images, and examples. As a graphic demonstration of this limiting process, consider the *limiting circles* shown below.

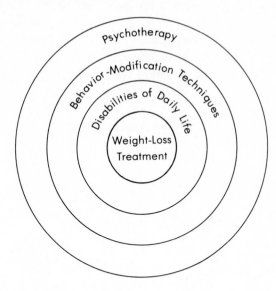

Notice how the writer has found more and more limited areas of the topic for purposes of an essay. Often one set of limiting circles still leaves too large and imponderable a topic for the writer. In such cases, the second set of limiting circles simply begins where the first one left off.

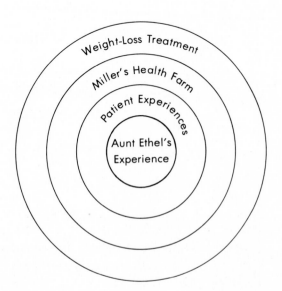

With such limiting circles, the writer boils down a topic into a manageable set of related ideas. The circles also help to keep the chosen ideas in context. The writer can easily see and make reference to the larger spheres of meaning lying outside the bounds of the limited topic.

Exercise 6.6   Using the circles provided, limit each of the large topics given in the outer circle.

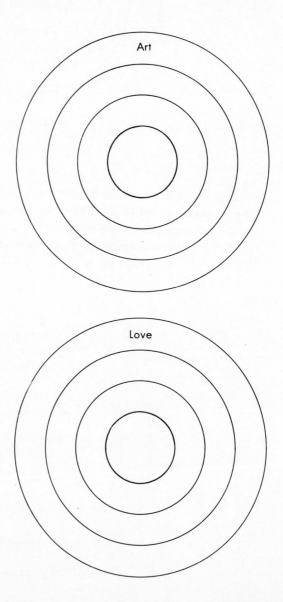

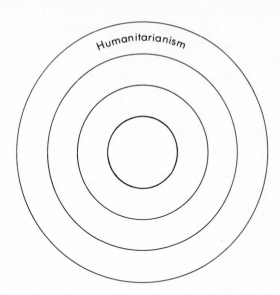

Stating the Topic Clearly

Once you have limited your area of interest, go on to state your topic with precision. This process can be visualized by using limiting circles again. Notice how the precise meaning of the inner-most limiting circle can be stated fully and clearly by referring to its context, the outer circles of meaning.

Stated clearly, the topic is *Best-Selling Spy Tales of the CIA.*

Exercise 6.7

For each of the limiting circles below, state the topic in a clear and complete way.

Topic: _____

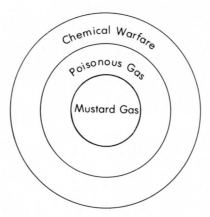

Topic: _____

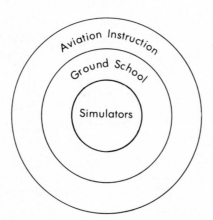

Topic: _____

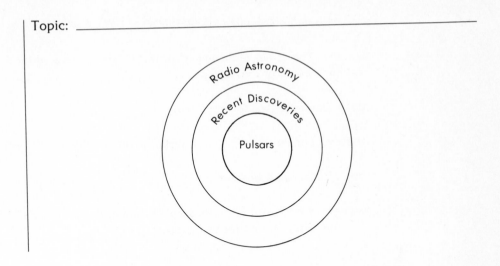

Converting the Topic into a Specific Problem

For deep and mysterious reasons, we are less interested in unchanging matters than we are in changing events, fortunes, and ideas. The headline, "Trucking in Winter," for example, attracts less interest than "Trucker Missing in Blizzard." The first headline is a *topic;* the second headline poses a *problem.* Topics may make us listen, but problems make us care.

We seem to inhabit an age and culture of problems. Almost by habit, we begin our day with an eye toward the problems and hurdles lying before us and how we are going to solve them: the problem of the sticking toaster, the problem of the crowded freeway. Necessarily, our essay patterns—the way we think and write—usually fall into this pattern of problem-solution thinking. Our readers expect the tension of the problem and the relief of the solution.

Some readers, in far different times and cultures, had no such expectation. They did not choose to perceive life as an endless series of problems. They did not define successful living as the ability to solve problems.

We necessarily write for a culture expecting problem-solution thinking. We do not, though, have to believe that life must be perceived in those terms, or should be.

Look at how the following three topics have been converted into problems.

TOPIC: Home Foreclosures in the 1980s

PROBLEM: The "creative financing" of the 1970s has created the foreclosure time bomb of the 1980s

TOPIC: Domestic Pets for the Elderly

PROBLEM: Loneliness and lack of responsibility are killing our elderly.

TOPIC: Endangered Species

PROBLEM: Your favorite ivory brooch and brand new alligator shoes may sign the death warrant for two species.

Notice the stultifying effect that topics have on the mind of the writer. What can be said about foreclosures, pets, and endangered species? So much *needs* to be said that nothing *can* be said. These large topics call to mind encyclopedias and textbooks, not essays.

Problems, by contrast, throw the mind into immediate, directed activity. Consider the problem, "The 'creative financing' of the 1970s has set the stage for the foreclosure time bomb of the 1980s." The writer can immediately set to work. What was creative financing? Why was it so prevalent in the 1970s? How has it set the stage for foreclosures in the 1980s? Problems inevitably lead reader and writer directly into the heart of the matter: What is the problem? Why is there a problem? Who suffers from the problem? How can the problem be solved?

Exercise 6.8   Convert each of the following topics into a specific problem.

1. Television

   _____

   _____

2. Violence in Sports

   _____

   _____

3. Anti-Americanism Abroad

_____

_____

4. Medicare

_____

_____

5. Rent Control

_____

_____

Certainly not all essays have to burn with the fervor of arguments and issues. A nature essay—"Cockroaches"—may simply want to report on the fascinating varieties, habits, and haunts of the bugs. Nevertheless, the essay will prove more involving and attractive to the reader if the topic Cockroaches is converted to a specific problem: "A Problem of Image: the Hated Cockroach." Once posed as a problem, the topic seems to open up for the writer: What is the cockroach's image? Why is the cockroach hated? Should it be hated? What might we admire about it?

Exercise 6.9

Convert each of the following noncontroversial topics into problems that are useful to the essayist and involving for the reader.

1. Rural Cabins

_____

_____

2. A College Degree

_____

_____

3. Goldfish

_____

_____

4. Darkness

5. Travel

6b(2)   Organizing the Essay

Up to this point, the writer has boiled down a workable topic, brainstormed about its possibilities, and shaped a specific problem from the topic. The next step in the architecture of the essay is choosing a pattern of organization. The end result of this step will be a working outline to guide the actual writing of the essay.

Each of the following paths describes a pattern of thought that is useful for organizing ideas, facts, and examples. The writer is always free to invent alternate paths or temporary detours, guided always by one principle: *let the path serve the purpose.* Don't take alleyways, that is to say, from New York City to Boston, if you intend to get there quickly.

Problem-Solution Pattern

This pattern of organization is one of the most useful for college essays and research papers. It defines a problem, then explores its roots and implications.

A. What is the problem?
B. How did the problem come to be?
C. What have others said or done about the problem?
D. How might the problem be resolved?
E. How would the future be changed if the problem were resolved?

Notice that each of these steps stimulates the writing of a paragraph. In a longer essay, more than one paragraph can be written for each step.

To illustrate the problem-solution pattern, we shall use the specific problem of Aunt Ethel's experience at Miller's Health Farm.

A. What is the problem?

In May of 1981, my Aunt Ethel Hasslewood lost a thousand dollars for every pound shed (she lost five) at the Miller Health Farm for the Obese. Although Miller's literature advertised "a clinically controlled environment to support the willpower of each visitor," Aunt Ethel found instead a staff getting rich off a carefully planned black market of sorts. Orderlies and groundskeepers let patients know from the start that chocolate bars, potato chips and even whole cakes and pies could be smuggled in for the right price. The price, of course, was wrong: $4 for a candy bar, $25 for a pie. In spite of her best intentions, Aunt Ethel gave in to such insidious temptations.

B. How did the problem come to be? (a paragraph explaining why Aunt Ethel sought out the farm)

C. What do others say about the problem? (the reaction of the farm administrators when Aunt Ethel refused to pay her bill)

D. How might the problem be resolved? (a paragraph offering possible ways to prevent the medically vulnerable from becoming prey to pirates)

E. How would the future be changed if the problem were solved? (a vision of medical treatment facilities that produce what they advertise—the paragraph may look forward to an Aunt Ethel who receives help instead of trickery)

Exercise 6.9

Using the concern described below, jot down the approximate content (as illustrated above) for each essay section. After doing so, choose one section and write out the entire paragraph as it might appear in the essay. (Leave the marginal boxes blank for the time being. They will be used in a later exercise.)

A. What is the problem?

Children are influenced by arcade games with a common theme: kill the enemy before the enemy kills you.

B. How did the problem come
    to be?

    _____

    _____

    _____

    _____

    _____

C. What do others say about the
    problem?

    _____

    _____

    _____

    _____

D. How might the problem be
    resolved?

    _____

    _____

    _____

    _____

E. How would the future be
    changed if the problem were
    solved?

    _____

    _____

    _____

    _____

Personal Viewpoint Pattern

In writing about a personal opinion or point of view, we look not to others but to ourselves—our own experiences, memories, thoughts, and feelings—for the substance of the essay. The personal viewpoint pattern helps the writer to organize personal thoughts, which otherwise have a way of rambling. Because the personal-viewpoint essay asks for our own attitudes and experiences, the use of *I, me,* and *we* is entirely proper.

A. How I used to view the problem
B. A memorable event, image, idea, or experience that changed my view
C. How I now view the problem
D. What action or feeling is now possible, given my new view?
E. My reflections, looking back over the change in my view

We will once again use Aunt Ethel's visit to Miller's to illustrate the pattern.

A. How I used to view the problem

> I used to laugh inside when overweight friends announced their impending visits to "fat farms." I was sure that it was the easiest thing in the world to maintain about 2 pounds of heft for each inch in height. I was 5 feet 8 inches tall, for example, and felt quite fit at 136 pounds. How ludicrous, I thought, to spend good money trying to buy what willpower alone could provide—simple, calm control over eating habits.

B. A memorable event, image, idea, or experience that changed my view (a paragraph telling of Aunt Ethel's sad experience at the health farm)
C. How I now view the problem (a paragraph describing the writer's new view that those seeking help for weight control are medically vulnerable)
D. What action or feeling is now possible, given my new view? (a paragraph discussing possible ways to license or monitor farms and clinics for the overweight)
E. My reflections, looking back over the change in my view (a paragraph admitting that the problems of others always seem simple until they touch close to home)

Exercise 6.10 | Jot down the approximate content of each of the following essay sections. Write out one paragraph in full. You may choose any section

(A–E) except that chosen in the previous exercise. (Leave the boxes blank.)

A. How I used to view the problem

Mountain climbing poses foolish

hazards for no productive

cause.

_____

_____

B. A memorable event, image, idea, or experience that changed my view

_____

_____

_____

_____

_____

C. How I now view the problem

_____

_____

_____

_____

D. What action or feeling is now possible, given my new view

_____

_____

_____

_____

E. My reflections, looking back
over the change in my view

Comparison/Contrast Pattern

This method of development and organization can prove useful in pointing out advantages and disadvantages between competing alternatives. The pattern helps to order many points in a persuasive way.

A. The problem may be addressed in at least two ways
B. Merits and flaws of the *least* attractive way
C. Flaws and merits of the *most* attractive way
D. How the most attractive way can be put into use
E. The bright future when the attractive way is in use

This pattern of development might well be used to argue for one course of action over another. Let's say, for example, that our essay deals with the question of attending graduate school.

PROBLEM: The desirability of a graduate education has to be weighed against salary considerations.

A. The problem may be addressed in at least two ways

College students thinking about high-technology careers face a difficult dilemma after they earn the B.A. or B.S. On one hand, they can choose to endure the poverty of student life for at least two more years while they pursue a graduate degree. On the other hand, they can begin working in the chosen field, settling for a graduate education made up of moonlight courses. The choice must be made each June, a time when stamina and financing are powerfully influential factors.

B. Merits and flaws of the *least* attractive way

Going to graduate school allows single-minded concentration on studies—(a merit)—and continuity from undergraduate studies—(another merit.) Unfortunately, (a flaw) also exists: the two years of "missed" salary may never be recovered in full, even though high-technology employees with advanced degrees earn somewhat more than those with only the B.A. or B.S.

C. Flaws and merits of the *most* attractive way

While coordinating studies with work means it takes longer to attain an advanced degree—(a flaw)—the student realizes distinct advantages. First, the employer usually pays for schooling. Second, the student has practical career goals in mind when arranging graduate programs and projects. Third, the student earns at least 85–90 percent as much during the first two years of employment as during the same period with an advanced degree. (All three advantages are merits.)

D. How the most attractive way can be put into use

Several companies offer work/study arrangements. Universities offer more and more evening classes for graduate students.

E. The bright future when the attractive way is in use

The day of full-time graduate students in high-technology fields of study may be over for most universities, unless they can attract the independently wealthy.

Observe a shift between sections B and C. In section B, the merits of the least attractive plan were given *prior* to the disadvantages. We wish to leave the reader with negative impressions of the least attractive way. But in turning to the most attractive way, we wish to dispense with the disadvantages first so that we can place final emphasis on the *merits* of the way.

Exercise 6.11 | For the problem cited below, jot down the approximate content of each section of the essay. Write out one paragraph of your choice (but not from the same section as those chosen in the previous two exercises. (Again, leave the boxes blank for now.)

PROBLEM: Working at an early age often instills a cynical attitude toward employment. Bosses can be abusive, intolerant, and too demanding toward adolescent workers.

A. The problem may be addressed in at least two ways

_____

_____

_____

_____

_____

B. Merits and flaws of the least attractive way

_____

_____

_____

_____

C. Flaws and merits of the most attractive way

_____

_____

_____

_____

D. How the most attractive way
can be put into use

_____

_____

_____

_____

_____

E. The bright future when the
attractive way is in use

_____

_____

_____

_____

_____

Social Viewpoint Pattern

This pattern offers a structure for examining public beliefs and opinions.
The pattern begins by defining conflicting viewpoints, then argues for the
viewpoint chosen by the writer.

A. The majority (or common) attitude
B. The minority (or uncommon) attitude
C. Evidence supporting the minority (uncommon) view
D. Obstacles to making the minority (uncommon) view more popular
E. Looking toward the future (a prediction or prognosis)

As an example of the social-viewpoint pattern, we may pose the following problem:

Paradoxically, science fiction looks backward more than forward. It may,
in fact, be a blinder on our efforts to foresee our actual future.

A. The majority attitude

Science fiction stories, books, and films are commonly thought to contain prophetic glimpses into the world of the future.

B. The minority attitude

Some people disagree. Science fiction, they argue, looks back to *former* cultural concerns, themes, beliefs, heroes, and villains.

C. Evidence supporting the minority view

When read closely, science fiction rehearses all the tired machinery of medieval romance: princes, princesses, lords, tyrants, invaders, kingdoms, battles, personal heroism, and courtly love.

D. Obstacles to making the minority view more popular

Perhaps the general reading public prefers not to look forward, choosing the predictable patterns of the past over a frightening future. The public, however, does want the *illusion* of looking into the future. Science fiction provides that illusion.

E. Looking toward the future

Science fiction will remain an immature art form so long as it holds itself out to be what it is not.

Exercise 6.12 For the problem cited below, jot down the approximate content of each section. Write out one paragraph in full. Do not choose a section used in previous exercises. (Leave the boxes blank.)

PROBLEM: While a host of social institutions have dedicated themselves to "saving" marriages, few groups offer help in ending bad marriages.

A. The majority view

_____

_____

_____

_____

_____

B. The minority view

_____

_____

_____

_____

_____

C. Evidence supporting the minority view

_____

_____

_____

_____

D. Obstacles to making the minority view more popular

_____

_____

_____

_____

E. Looking toward the future

_____

_____

_____

_____

By following such purposeful paths of argument, the architecture of the essay becomes clear to both writer and reader. Only one planning step remains before the writing of the rough draft begins.

6b(3) Choosing Details and Examples

Readers love details and examples. Abstract assertions, such as "Art involves contrast," gain life when the writer adds an explanatory detail or example: ". . . as, for example, the yielding of hard stone to the soft, flowing form of the Venus de Milo." Only rarely does a writer include too many details and examples. More often, the reader is left wishing for more specific illustrations as the writer plunges ahead into abstraction. In the example below, notice how the beginning abstraction is clarified and imaginatively "brought home" by its accompanying example.

> War often involves small dramas of conscience. Several Air Force fighter pilots, after service in Viet Nam, admitted dropping napalm bombs miles away from their authorized targets. The intended sites, the pilots knew, were populated with as many friends as foes.

We have only a limited capacity to view airy abstractions with much caring. By contrast, we have an almost boundless ability to imagine the sights, sounds, smells, and predicaments of actual living. Writers draw upon this powerful resource when they include frequent details and examples.

What makes a good example? In their best examples, writers create the "feel" of reality by specifying actual details, not broad generalizations.

NOT: A man once lost his pet, only to discover it later in another part of the house.

INSTEAD: Last May Brian Jenkins of Portland lost his pet boa constrictor, only to discover it two weeks later safe and snug under his mattress.

Notice the additions we made:

Who? (Jenkins of Portland, not "a man")
When? (last May, not "once")
What? (lost his pet boa constrictor, not "his pet")
How? (discovered it "safe and snug")
Where? (under his mattress, not "in another part of the house")

Exercise 6.13 | Convert each of the poor examples below into vivid examples by specifying exact details for such questions as who? when? what? how? where? and perhaps even why? You may often choose to omit one or more of these questions.

1. U.S. students performed a charitable act in Mexico after the bad weather there.

   _____

   _____

   _____

2. Her car had been customized in an attractive way.

   _____

   _____

   _____

3. His clothing made a good impression on those gathered at the meeting.

   _____

   _____

   _____

4. The music helped calm the crowd after the leader's announcement.

   _____

   _____

   _____

After discovering good examples, writers must decide where those examples belong. As a general rule, add examples or details wherever they will help your reader grasp the significance of your point. Examples are especially appropriate after abstract assertions that pose difficulties or ambiguities for the reader.

You can plan in advance just where examples and details belong on the "blue-print" of your essay. In the case of our earlier practice essay on

Miller's Health Farm, appropriate examples might be indicated in the following manner:

A. What is the problem?

Some "health farms" are designed to steal from patients.

EXAMPLE: Aunt Ethel's experience
   DETAIL: Candy bar black market
   DETAIL: Outrageous prices

B. How did the problem come to be?

Efforts of obese people to borrow strength from others

EXAMPLE: Aunt Ethel's many attempts to lose weight
   DETAIL: Pills
   DETAIL: Hypnotism
   DETAIL: Exercise

The map of examples and details would be completed for all sections of the essay.

Exercise 6.14 | Go back to the essay frameworks you developed in exercises 6.9–6.12. In the blank boxes, place an example with two or more supporting details. You may not wish to fill each box. You must decide which of your points needs clarification through examples and details.

The essay blueprint on pages 136–137 summarizes the steps of mental preparation, architectural planning, and organization of the essay. By using the essay blueprint, you will develop a *working outline* for writing your essay. Choose from the topics below, then proceed step by step through the essay blueprint sheet.

TOPICS: Hair styles   Fire   Gangs   Weather   Gardening   Dreams

(your choice: _____)

6c The First Draft

By working through the essay blueprint, you have provided yourself with a *working outline* for writing the *first draft* of your essay. In Appendix B, an

ESSAY BLUEPRINT

A Checklist for Mental Preparation

1. Clear the decks.
2. Attack the essay as a challenge.
3. Avoid the panic of deadlines.

KNOW YOURSELF: Who are you? How do you sound in writing? Are you ready to be yourself?
Your voice counts. Use it.

KNOW YOUR AUDIENCE: To whom are you writing? How do you feel about them? How do they feel about you?
Your audience wants to understand. Help them.

KNOW YOUR TOPIC: Select a topic that interests you and generate ideas through brainstorming.

Twelve Brainstorms	*Jottings*
1. If no one (or everyone) had _____ , how would the world be different?	_____
2. What kind of people find _____ especially tempting, interesting, or valuable? Why?	_____
3. For certain periods of my life, I was almost unaware (or particularly aware) of _____ . Why?	_____
4. _____ is/are usually associated with a certain part of the world. Why?	_____
5. Few (many) people lie awake at night thinking about _____ . Why?	_____
6. _____ can have an impact upon emotions. How?	_____
7. _____ , in spite of its surface simplicity, has/have a deeper significance. What is it?	_____
8. _____ arouse(s) widely different memories. What are they?	_____
9. _____ can be divided into major parts. What are they?	_____
10. _____ might be wholly unnecessary if. . .	_____
11. _____ is not the way it was in the past. Why?	_____
12. When I think of _____ , three images come to mind. Why? What are they?	_____

A Checklist for Architectural Planning

1. Define your topic by circling your most promising ideas about it.
2. Limit your topic by using limiting circles.
3. Now specify your limited topic: _____ .

ESSAY BLUEPRINT

Essay Patterns

Choose or invent an essay pattern suitable for your topic-problem.

1. Problem-Solution	*2. Personal Viewpoint*	*3. Compare/Contrast*	*4. Social Viewpoint*
A. The problem	A. Once I felt . . .	A. Two ways to go	A. Majority view
B. Its history or source	B. Something happened	B. The pros and cons of the worst way	B. Minority view
C. What others say or have tried	C. Now I feel . . .	C. The cons and pros of the best way	C. Support for minority view
D. What needs to be tried	D. Now I can or will . . .	D. Implementing the best way	D. Obstacles to minority view
E. The future	E. Looking back, I see . . .	E. The future . . .	E. Looking ahead . . .

Essay topic: _____

Stated as a *problem:* _____

_____

Pattern _____   Details

A. _____   _____

_____   _____

_____   _____

B. _____   _____

_____   _____

_____   _____

C. _____   _____

_____   _____

_____   _____

D. _____   _____

_____   _____

_____   _____

E. _____   _____

_____   _____

_____   _____

essay blueprint has been completed as an example of the development we have discussed. Take the time to compare the bare bones of the essay in Appendix B with the outline you have developed for your essay.

The architecture—the blueprint—of your essay lies before you, finished now as a working outline. You are ready to turn the outline, with its brief phrases and jottings, into a first draft. As an example of the process you are undertaking, let's consider how a sample from the essay blueprint can be changed into a paragraph in the first draft. You can see in Appendix B how a complete first draft grows out of the essay blueprint.

Essay topic, <u>Unwed Fathers</u>, stated as a problem: <u>Unwed fathers can</u>

<u>suffer psychological damage.</u>

Pattern: <u>Personal viewpoint</u>   Details/Examples

A. <u>Once I felt that unwed fathers got off</u>   1. President of class in h.s.

<u>scot-free.</u>   2. Minister's daughter

To write the first paragraph of the first draft, we can begin by expressing the thought in section A in a complete way. Then, following our paragraph models from Chapters 2–4, we can expand, illustrate, and conclude the paragraph as follows:

[1] Main idea

[2] Expansion

[3] Illustration

[4] Conclusion—
"So what?"

[1] Especially during high school years, I felt that unwed fathers walked away unscarred from the accident of a child's birth. [2] Teen-age mothers were left behind with hard decisions and lifelong responsibilities. [3] When the president of my high school senior class learned he was to be an unwed father, he expressed deep remorse—and then went on to college and a successful life. The mother and child still live with her parents. In another example from those years, my minister's only daughter found herself pregnant at seventeen. Her father wanted nothing to do with her boyfriend, and insisted that she never see him again. That verdict suited the scared young father well: he left the scene of the accident seemingly unscarred. [4] How unfair, I thought, that the trauma and anxiety of such difficult experiences have to be borne by the mother alone.

While no writer can avoid the work that goes into hard thinking and careful writing, three suggestions may help save time and effort.

Let yourself write with confidence. You recognize that much in your first draft will not be perfect. At the same time, you also know that much will be not only usable, but also quite good. You are seeking the gold and silver of fine writing in the unrefined ore of the first draft.

Write with continuity. Try to set aside a block of time in which you can write the first draft beginning to end. If your essay is too long or your time too short for this approach, at least try to set aside substantial amounts of uninterrupted time for writing. In the act of composition, your thoughts are concentrated on your material like a hot, white light. In that heat of creation you write freely, naturally, and successfully. By contrast, a series of ten-minute writing sessions inevitably produces a patchwork essay of disjointed thoughts. The seams show.

Write with conviction. To a remarkable extent, your readers will follow your lead. Your involvement with your topic is contagious.

Exercise 6.15 | You have already chosen a topic from among this group:

Hair Styles   Fire   Gangs   Weather   Gardening   Dreams

(your choice: _____)

By using the essay blueprint sheet, you have created a working outline for an essay, complete with examples and details. Now follow that outline to write the first draft of your essay.

6d   The Polished Essay

You have created a first draft, probably in handwritten form, with many cross-outs. We will now describe the processes by which the first draft can reach its final form as a polished essay.

6d(1)   Eliminating Unnecessary Words

As you reread your first draft, you may notice that some words and sentences swerve away from your main point. Circle such words and sentences for removal. An example of this process appears in Appendix B. Notice how each circled word and phrase there is unnecessary to the main point of the paragraph at hand.

Usually, unnecessary words can be recognized by the following characteristics.

1. Some words echo the meaning of an accompanying word.

    She trusted in (false) illusions.

    SOLUTION: Remove "false."

2. Some words have little or no meaning at all.

    (It) (was) the governor (who) finally brought the senator to his senses.

    SOLUTION: Remove the circled words.

3. Some words, phrases, and sentences lead the reader away from your main point.

    Nuclear power continues to provoke controversy on college campuses. (Although my brother's college has never had a demonstration,) twelve of the nation's twenty largest universities have had to call out police this year to contain antinuclear gatherings.

    SOLUTION: Remove the circled words.

Exercise 6.16 Circle the unnecessary words in the following sentences.

1. These gases often occur in the environment of the upper atmosphere.
2. Children with special talents, abilities, and gifts should receive additional attention through extra supplemental programs and activities.
3. In old age as a senior citizen, Martinelli owed his good spirits to the game of baseball.
4. There were six men who knew the location and whereabouts of the kidnapped child being held for ransom by the kidnappers.
5. The jury foreman answered with an affirmative response, "yes," when the judge in charge asked if the jury had reached a verdict.

6d(2) Checking for Logical Connections

Reread your first draft for smooth, logical connections between thoughts, sentences, and paragraphs. These connections, or *transitions,* can be supplied by transitional words and by using similar subjects for thought transitions.

Transitional Words

Used with discretion, the following words can be helpful "traffic signs" to your readers. They signal sudden turns (*however*), new departures (*in addition*) and many other directional cues to understanding.

but	still	in short	inevitably
yet	because	in sum	consequently
however	although	in brief	gradually
furthermore	thus	first, second, finally	increasingly
therefore	hence	by contrast	more and more
similarly	nevertheless	of course	for example
in addition	in addition	for instance	probably

Usually transitional, traffic-sign words are not found at the end of the sentence; the traffic (your sentence) has already gone by.

NOT: The bisque-headed doll caused a flurry of excitement among collectors, <u>however</u>.

INSTEAD: The bisque-headed doll, <u>however</u>, caused a flurry of excitement among the collectors.

Often, transitional words occupy the position right after the subject.

The train, <u>of course</u>, outpaced the speeding car.
Five oil portraits, <u>therefore</u>, fell into his hands.
A sleazy nightclub, <u>after all</u>, raised eyebrows.

Occasionally, the transitional word occupies the initial strong slot in a sentence, especially when a traffic signal is crucial to the meaning of the sentence.

<u>Nevertheless</u>, Maxie pressed on.

Exercise 6.17 | Insert transitional words of your choice in each of the following sentences.

1. Pay TV attracted the audience courted so long by movie theatres.

_____

_____

2. Four backhoes were able to dig the holes for the bank's massive footings in less than a week.

_____

_____

3. The thermostat was set at 74 degrees.

_____

_____

4. A tomb-rubbing is free from all signs of morbidity.

_____

_____

5. Cold roofing compounds took the place of traditional hot-tar applications.

_____

_____

Probably you will not want to use transitional words in every sentence of an essay, any more than you would want to see too many traffic signs cluttering one street. Many writers avoid using transitional words in more than two sentences in a row.

Similar Subjects for Thought Transitions

Often two or three sentences can flow smoothly from one to the next when they begin with similar, but not identical, subjects.

DON'T USE AN IDENTICAL SUBJECT: <u>Board games</u> remain America's most popular indoor activity for young and old. <u>Board games</u>, even in inflationary times, remain inexpensive. <u>Board games</u> provide an alternative to television and video games for the family.

INSTEAD, USE SUBJECTS WITH SIMILAR MEANINGS: <u>Board games</u> remain America's most popular indoor activity for young and old. <u>Chess, checkers, and Monopoly</u>, even in inflationary times, remain inexpensive. <u>Such diversions</u> provide an alternative to television and video games for the family.

Exercise 6.18 | Write two similar substitutes for each of the following subjects.

1. Domesticated birds _____ _____

2. Prisoner _____ _____

3. Leisure time _____ _____

6d(3) Testing Diction for Power and Propriety

Diction refers to your choice of words. Reread your first draft, testing each of the words for power and propriety. In the case of nouns, be as specific as possible. Fill your verbs with vivid action. In the case of adjectives and adverbs, let your language be as crisp and descriptive as possible, in keeping with the overall purpose of your essay.

Consider the *connotations* of your words. A word's connotations are its overtones and associations; its explicit dictionary meaning is its *denotation*. *Mother* denotes the female parent, but connotes love and care.

NOT: Security measures were established to maintain the well-being of the
vague   *impersonal*   *stiff*

important guests at the civic occasion.
vague   *vague*

INSTEAD: The mayor instructed seven plain-clothes police officers to guard the governor's every move at the dedication of City Hall.

Exercise 6.19 | Rewrite the following sentences, making each of the underlined words more specific.

1. An <u>attractive decoration</u> topped the coach's birthday cake.

_____

_____

2. He opened the closet, only to see <u>a mess</u>.

_____

_____

3. Inside the can of beans they found a <u>coin</u>.

_____

_____

Rewrite the following sentences, adjusting the connotations of the underlined words.

1. Kris felt tears of happiness when her father proudly led her Christmas gift from the barn—a <u>nag</u>.

_____

_____

2. The personnel manager asked the applicant to have a seat in the first <u>stall</u>.

_____

_____

3. Brushing her cheek with his own, Jacques complimented Marie on the <u>odor</u> of her perfume.

_____

_____

Rewrite the following sentences, substituting vivid verbs for the underlined words.

1. The armored boat <u>made</u> its way through the ice.

_____

_____

2. Nine alley cats <u>produced sounds</u> behind the fish market.

_____

_____

3. After decades of separation, the old Corsican <u>greeted</u> his younger brother.

_____

_____

6d(4) Checking Errors in Logic

In conversations with friends we have all had occasion to say, "But that doesn't make sense!" Essays, too, can fail to make sense when they contain flaws in logic. Acquaint yourself with the eight most common logic errors in college writing. Watch for these flaws as you polish and revise your first draft.

1. *Hasty generalization:* a conclusion based on too little evidence.

    EXAMPLE: All Studebakers are steady brakers. I know; my brother owns one.

2. *Circular reasoning:* a purported explanation of an idea that merely restates the idea.

    EXAMPLE: We like to climb mountains because we love to hike to the top of huge, natural formations.

3. *Personal attack:* basing judgments about issues on estimates of personalities.

    EXAMPLE: The president's tax reforms are doomed to failure. How can a man who collects stamps ever understand the hard realities of the financial world?

4. *Non sequitur:* a conclusion that does not follow from the evidence.

    EXAMPLE: Harry probably got fired for losing his temper. He is half-Irish, you know.

5. *Either/or thinking:* two alternatives posed as the *only* alternatives.

    EXAMPLE: Either this nation must establish a powerful military presence on Tahiti or it will lose influence over the South Pacific.

6. *Straw man:* attacking a fabricated version of the opponent's position.

    EXAMPLE: Democrats are big spenders. Here in Minnesota we know how we feel about big spenders.

7. *False cause:* falsely taking an earlier event for the *cause* of a later event.

    EXAMPLE: The Yankees had a new general manager this year. No wonder they failed to make the playoffs.

8. *Stacking the argument:* amassing evidence favoring one side of the issue, while ignoring obvious evidence on the other side of the issue.

> EXAMPLE: John doesn't deserve a scholarship. Despite his academic record, his reputation reveals numerous personality clashes with professors. His College Board Test scores show that he is not equally bright in all areas. His senior essay was not universally admired by the faculty.

6d(5) Checking for Mechanical Errors

Like diamonds in the rough, fine essays can be overlooked or undervalued by readers who see only a profusion of mechanical errors. An important part of the polishing stage in writing is checking for mechanical errors *until there are none.* At first, you may wish to use the following checklist as a guide to your inspection of the first draft. Later, you will know what to look for without the necessity of working step by step through the checklist.

Check Item	*See This Source for Help*
Spelling	Appendix A and your dictionary
Sentence fragments	Chapter 7
Run-on sentences	Chapter 8
Comma splices	Chapter 8
Dangling sentence parts	Chapter 9
Subject-verb agreement	Chapter 10
Correct parts of verbs	Chapter 10
Pronoun agreement	Chapter 11
Pronoun form	Chapter 11
Comma uses	Chapter 12
Semicolon uses	Chapter 13
Colon uses	Chapter 13
Apostrophe uses	Chapter 14
Quotation marks	Chapter 14
Italics	Chapter 14
Dashes	Chapter 15
Parentheses	Chapter 15
Hyphens	Chapter 15
Capitalization	Chapter 16

6d(6) Making Stylistic Improvements

Finally, reread your first draft with an eye toward stylistic improvements based on the fifteen matters of style treated in Chapter 5. For your convenience, they are restated here in checklist form. Be sure to check back in Chapter 5 when you are unsure of the meaning of any of these items.

Check Item	See This Section
Using the active voice	5b
Varying sentence types	5c
Emphasizing important words through placement	5d
Being specific	5e
Eliminating wordiness	5f
Creating parallels	5g
Choosing pronouns	5h
Controlling paragraph length	5i
Avoiding trite and slang expressions	5j
Avoiding a posed and overwritten style	5k
Avoiding contractions and abbreviations	5l
Using parentheses correctly	5m
Avoiding unnecessary questions	5n
Choosing words carefully	5o
Avoiding awkward constructions and repetitions	5p

6d(7) Putting It All Together

A physician giving you a general examination may in fact be looking for hundreds of signs of bodily health or illness. Your doctor does not, however, work from a literal checklist of 306 symptoms, laboriously checking them off item by item. In a similar way, a sculptor may have dozens of internal artistic standards at work when trimming, texturing, pinching, and poking the final form of a clay figure. The sculptor's standards, though, are not applied in a strict 1-2-3 order.

When we polish the first draft of an essay, we revise more on the basis of a reservoir of writing concerns than according to a strict checklist. Beginning writers, however, often find it helpful to review the contents of such a checklist, even if they then set it aside. With practice, the process of polishing a first draft can be as spontaneous as the act of writing itself. The writer obeys no particular checklist, but instead reaches for the polishing tool that fits the task at hand.

Finally, then, you hold in your hand an essay ready for others to read. You have worked hard to bring it to its present polished state. Now, like an inventor testing a pet project for the first time, you will have the experience of seeing the essay *work*. You will hear your readers' responses to what you have written. Praise, of course, is always welcome. But good writers also learn the value of their readers' objections. Where was the essay difficult to grasp, and why? At what point did boredom set in? What additional details and examples could have clarified obscure points?

Often, comments from readers—especially professors—will lead to further revisions, based on the process discussed in Chapter 6d(1–6). This effort to clarify and perfect the essay pays a substantial dividend. Through clear writing, Sir Philip Sydney wrote, "we lend our minds out" to others. We express deeply and fully who we are, what we think, and what we feel.

Recap

1. Prepare for writing an essay by knowing yourself, knowing your audience, and knowing your topic.
2. Develop ideas, images, and examples for your essay by brainstorming.
3. Limit your essay topic to a specific area of concern.
4. State your topic clearly as a problem to be solved.
5. Choose or invent a pattern of organization for your essay. Four useful patterns are discussed in this chapter.
6. Using the "Essay Blueprint," create a working outline of your ideas and details for the essay.
7. Follow your outline in writing the rough draft.
8. Polish your rough draft in these ways:
   Eliminate unnecessary words.
   Check for logical connections.
   Test diction for power and propriety.
   Check for errors in logic.
   Check for mechanical and grammatical errors.
   Make stylistic improvements.

Writing Topics: The Essay

In writing essays about each of the following topics, address your remarks to the general reading public.

1. *Nice Day, But Cool*

Why, in all parts of the world, do people like to discuss the weather at such length? Write an essay on this fascination.

2. *The Jerk*

We inevitably encounter an occasional unpleasant person in daily life. Write an essay in which you discuss ways to deal with unpleasant people.

3. *Starting Over*

Particularly in moments of discouragement we fantasize about starting over in a new part of the world. Write an essay about this kind of escape.

4. *The Purple People*

Imagine a religious or social group whose members dyed their skin bright purple. Write an essay in which you discuss the kinds of resistance and obstacles such a group might encounter in your locale.

5. *The Five O'Clock Senator*

Television news personalities find it easy to launch political careers. Write an essay in which you discuss the dangers of using a television career as a steppingstone to politics.

6. *Tea Time*

Some cultures have raised simple acts such as the pouring of tea to the level of ritual. Write an essay in which you discuss some rituals of American life.

7. *Trash or Treasure*

The creations of many present-day poets, artists, and composers are not greeted with enthusiasm by the public. Write an essay in which you describe and analyze your own attitudes and responses toward modern poetry, art, or music.

8. Unshakably Me

We can be aware of many sides to an issue without giving up firm opinions and beliefs. Write an essay in which you explain and defend one of your firmly held beliefs.

9. No Justice

Life is not always fair. Write an essay in which you discuss reasonable ways of dealing with one or more personal or social injustices.

10. Blue Ribbon

We each have at least one thing that we do well. Write an essay in which you discuss one of your talents. Focus first on the obstacles you may have faced in reaching your potential, then on the inner qualities or outer circumstances that helped your talent blossom.

Other Essay Topics

11. Overcoming an Injury or Illness
12. Reducing Frustration
13. Fashion Fads
14. Grade Inflation
15. The Long Effects of Childhood Experiences
16. Sexual Roles and Stereotypes
17. The Future of Big Cities
18. The Problems of Competition
19. A Meaningful College Education
20. The Changing Nature of the Family
21. Advertising Trickery
22. Finding Friends
23. Fighting Anxieties
24. Honesty in Relationships
25. The Quality of Television
26. The Difficulty of Making Career Decisions
27. Remnants of Racism
28. The Rising Cost of Living
29. Parental Pressures
30. What High School Failed to Teach

PART TWO

A Guide to Grammar and Mechanics

The "rules" of good writing are more accurately referred to as the "conventions" of Standard Written English. Conventions are simply notions that people generally agree on. It is conventional, for example, for men to wear jackets and ties at fancy restaurants. Jackets and ties, of course, are not necessarily more beautiful or comfortable than football jerseys or sheepskin vests. But in certain places, formal wear has tradition and general opinion on its side. It seems the right thing to wear because people believe it's right.

When writing in schools, businesses, and the professions, educated people follow the conventions of Standard Written English. Like the conventions of dress, the conventions of writing reflect the general beliefs of people. Not following appropriate conventions in writing is comparable to wearing a football jersey to a fancy restaurant. It's not immoral. It's not less comfortable. It's simply not appropriate for the occasion. In addition, many of the conventions of Standard Written English also follow logic and common sense. Writers who violate the conventions may appear illogical and may fail to communicate effectively to their audience.

You will *want* people to accept and value your writing, especially in your academic and career undertakings. Toward that end, this text will remind you what the conventions of Standard Written English are. You will find practical hints and a great deal of practice in patterns of punctuation, grammar, and usage. Through such exercises, you can master the most important conventions of Standard Written English. Then, along with your favorite football jersey, you will have one more suit of clothes to put on when you want to and need to.

This portion of the text may be used in several ways. Its arrangement reflects the authors' belief that some skills in grammar and mechanics are more fundamental than others and should be reviewed and mastered first. Thus, some instructors may wish their classes to proceed through Part Two in sequence. Others may wish to assign portions of it in connection with assignments in Part One. Still others may decide to use it selectively, based on the results of pretests or in response to specific problems as they arise in writing. Part Two also will be a handy reference whenever you have a question about grammar or mechanics.

Chapter 7

Complete Sentences

Writing in complete sentences is one of the most important conventions of Standard Written English. It is possible to give a grammatical definition of a complete sentence, such as, "A grammatically complete sentence consists of a subject and a predicate." It is also possible to try to define a complete sentence in terms of its meaning by saying, for example, that a sentence must "express a complete thought" or that it must be able to "stand alone." This chapter will give you practice in recognizing groups of words that are not complete sentences, usually called "fragments" or "incomplete sentences," and in converting them to whole sentences.

Pretest: Complete Sentences

Identify each group of words below as a complete sentence (OK) or a fragment (F). Rewrite fragments to make them complete sentences.

_____ 1. The wind blows hard in western Afghanistan.

_____

_____

_____ 2. Often reaching 100 miles an hour.

_____

_____ 3. Sweeping south from the Kyzyl-Kum steppes of inner Asia, a torrid gale known locally as "the wind that kills cows."

_____

_____

_____ 4. Often reaching 100 miles an hour, this wind blows hardest in Seistan.

_____

_____

_____ 5. A dry, hot region that extends across Afghanistan's southwestern border into Iran.

_____

_____

_____ 6. Seistanis were the first people to channel the wind's wild energy into work.

_____

_____

_____ 7. During the ninth century or before, Seistanis invented the windmill.

_____

_____

_____ 8. Inspired by horizontal, wind-driven prayer wheels that whirled in Tibet and Mongolia at least as late as one hundred years ago.

_____

_____

_____ 9. The sails of the initial Seistani mills almost certainly rotated horizontally, like the millstone.

_____

_____

_____ 10. Thus bypassing the need for a gear to translate vertical into horizontal torque.

_____

_____

7a   The Parts of a Sentence

Understanding a few basic grammatical terms makes it easier to talk about and solve problems with fragments. These terms are *clause, phrase,* and *sentence,* as well as *subject* and *predicate.*

A *clause* is a group of words consisting of a *subject* and a *predicate.* There are two types of clauses: *independent* clauses (also called *main* clauses) and *dependent* clauses (also called *subordinate* clauses).

An *independent clause* may stand alone as a complete sentence.

The telephone rang.
   Subject   *Predicate*

A clerk picked up the receipt.
  Subject   *Predicate*

To identify the subject of a clause, ask *who* or *what* performs the action indicated by the predicate. For instance, for the preceding examples we might ask, "What rang?" The answer, *the telephone,* correctly identifies the subject. The answer to the question, "Who picked up the receipt?" identifies the subject of the second example, *a clerk.*

The predicate of *The telephone rang* consists of a single verb, *rang.* In *A clerk picked up the receipt,* the predicate consists of the verb (*picked up*) and the other words related to it, *the receipt.*

A *dependent clause* contains a subject and a predicate, but it cannot stand alone as an independent clause can.

because the switchboard was overloaded
     Subject   *Predicate*

until the committee meeting adjourned
     Subject   *Predicate*

The first example gives a reason for something else, but it does not itself express a complete thought. It must be part of a larger sentence:

I couldn't call you because the switchboard was overloaded.

The complete sentence now contains an independent clause, *I couldn't call you,* and a dependent clause, *because the switchboard was overloaded.* The two clauses together express a complete thought.

The second example, too, needs to be combined with an independent clause to make a complete sentence:

Everyone waited nervously until the committee adjourned.

The dependent clause, *until the committee adjourned,* is only part of the complete sentence. In this case, it explains how long everyone waited nervously.

    A *sentence* consists of at least one independent clause. A *simple sentence* contains only one independent clause. In writing, a sentence begins with a capital letter and ends with a period, question mark, or exclamation mark.

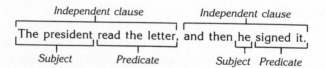

Compound sentences consist of more than one independent clause joined by a *coordinating conjunction* such as *and, or, but,* and *yet.*

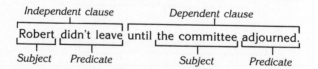

Complex sentences consist of one or more independent clauses and one or more dependent clauses joined by a *subordinating conjunction* such as *until, because, since, when,* and *while.*

Independent clause | Dependent clause

Robert didn't leave | until the committee adjourned.

Subject | Predicate | Subject | Predicate

    A *phrase* is a group of words that lacks a subject or predicate. There are three main kinds of phrases.

    A *prepositional phrase* consists of a preposition (a word like *at, by, except, for, from, in, of, on, to, under,* or *until*) followed by a noun or pronoun, which is called its object.

Children swam *in the pool.*

We met *after lunch.*

Bill borrowed the keys *from her.*

The office sent a check *to him.*

In, after, from, and *to* are prepositions. *Pool, lunch, her,* and *him* are objects of those prepositions.

A *noun phrase* consists of a main noun, called the headword, plus all of the other words that modify or describe it.

That tall, well-dressed man asked for you again.

They discovered a *splendid collection of silver coins.*

The nouns that are the headwords in these noun phrases are *man* and *collection.*

A *verbal phrase* consists of a verb plus various other words that go with it to form a unit. There are many different kinds of verbal phrases, but it is not necessary to know the names of all of them to solve the common writing problems that involve such phrases.

Reading by candlelight strained her eyes.

Sharon demanded *to see the manager.*

The rabbit *hopping in our garden* belongs to Hank.

Blown down by the wind, our garage was a total loss.

Each phrase above has a verb form as its headword: *reading, to see, hopping, blown.*

7b Avoiding Fragments by Combining with Complete Sentences

Whenever a phrase or a dependent clause is written as if it were a sentence, that is, beginning with a capital letter and ending with a period, question mark, or exclamation mark, such a phrase or clause is called a *fragment* or an *incomplete sentence.*

In the first example, a dependent clause is incorrectly punctuated as a complete sentence. This dependent clause must be included as part of a sentence with an independent clause.

FRAGMENT: Because it ran out of gas.

OK: The car stopped because it ran out of gas.

The fragment below is a prepositional phrase that lacks both subject and predicate. In can be rewritten correctly as part of a complete sentence.

FRAGMENT: Throughout the entire westside neighborhood.

OK: New building was going on throughout the entire westside neighborhood.

In the next fragment, a noun phrase stands alone without a predicate. Adding a predicate to it will form a complete sentence.

FRAGMENT: A remarkably preserved ship lying in deep water three miles off-shore.

OK: A remarkably preserved ship lying in deep water three miles offshore recently became the subject of an international research project.

The verbal phrase that follows is not a complete sentence by itself, but it can be made part of a complete sentence.

FRAGMENT: Calling on all citizens for assistance.

OK: The Neighborhood Cleanup Committee is calling on all citizens for assistance.

In each of the following examples, a complete sentence is followed by a fragment. The sentence and the fragment are then combined to make a single whole sentence.

INCORRECT: The arctic is a hostile environment. Where frigid, desert-dry winds race across the ice.

CORRECT: The arctic is a hostile environment where frigid, desert-dry winds race across the ice.

INCORRECT: The plants that have adapted to the arctic are abundant. Although the inhospitable climate has limited the number of species.

CORRECT: The plants that have adapted to the arctic are abundant, although the inhospitable climate has limited the number of species.

Exercise 7.1 | Combine the following whole sentences and fragments to make a single complete sentence.

1. Arctic plants have penetrated one of the earth's most hostile environments. By crowding together and staying close to their roots.

   _____

   _____

   _____

2. Many plants in the ecosystem are covered with hairs. Not only to keep them warm, but also to reduce the drying effects of the wind.

   _____

   _____

   _____

3. In the extremely cold climate, trees are only able to produce wood close to the ground. Where it is often warmer.

   _____

   _____

   _____

4. In cold-water habitats, certain fish and invertebrates convert starches into complex carbohydrates called glycerols. In effect manufacturing their own antifreeze.

   _____

   _____

   _____

5. Climatologists consider much of the arctic a polar desert. Because it receives less than ten inches of precipitation a year.

   _____

   _____

   _____

6. Moisture is locked up in the permafrost. Frozen soil that is rock hard and may reach half a mile in depth.

_____

_____

_____

7. Nearly all flowering plants in the arctic are perennial. Which means they live through more than a single season.

_____

_____

_____

8. Some plants, like the evergreens, keep the same leaves for several years. To save energy.

_____

_____

_____

9. The blossoms of some plants, like the yellow or white arctic poppies, swivel to follow the sun. Thereby acting as parabolas that concentrate the sun's heat on the plants' reproductive parts.

_____

_____

_____

10. Human technology is quickly spreading through the arctic region. Threatening the delicate balance of life that has evolved here.

_____

_____

_____

7c Avoiding Fragments by Adding or Altering a Verb

Each of the following two examples shows a fragment and how it can be converted into a complete sentence. Words added or altered are italicized.

FRAGMENT: Many old-time stoves made of cast iron sections rather loosely joined together with screws or bolts.

OK: *Stovesmiths made* many old-time stoves of cast iron sections rather loosely joined together with screws or bolts.

FRAGMENT: The era of cheap energy coming to an abrupt end in 1973.

OK: The era of cheap energy *came* to an abrupt end in 1973.

Exercise 7.2   Convert the following fragments into complete sentences, making as few changes as possible.

1. The fact being that fewer than 200,000 wood stoves had been sold in the year before the oil embargo.

    _____

    _____

    _____

2. By 1975, the number more than doubling, to 407,000.

    _____

    _____

    _____

3. By the end of the 1970s, more than one million residential wood stoves being sold per year.

    _____

    _____

    _____

4. A wood stove, symbol of its owner's desire to slash home-heating bills with one grand gesture.

    _____

    _____

    _____

5. The best type of stove being the "airtight" variety.

_____

_____

_____

6. With only enough air to sustain the fire, the fuel surrendering more heat.

_____

_____

_____

7. The result, a load of wood burns longer and your costs for wood are correspondingly less.

_____

_____

_____

8. The hallmark of an airtight stove, a tight fitting door and an air inlet that can throttle down the fire.

_____

_____

_____

9. The question remaining whether you need a wood stove to help lower your home-heating costs.

_____

_____

_____

10. Thrifty or not, stoves often appealing to our nostalgia for simpler times.

_____

_____

_____

7d Avoiding Fragments by Combining with Complete Sentences or Rewriting

In each of the following examples there is a fragment. The fragment is combined with the preceding sentence to make one complete sentence.

INCORRECT: During the mid-thirteenth century, King Henry III possessed a huge white bear. *Whose upkeep was very expensive.*

CORRECT: During the mid-thirteenth century, King Henry III possessed a huge white bear whose upkeep was very expensive.

INCORRECT: This extravagant pet was led to the river by its keeper each day. *Fishing for its own food.*

CORRECT: This extravagant pet was led to the river each day by its keeper to fish for its own food.

INCORRECT: *A huge white bear ambling down the street.* This was a sight to behold.

CORRECT: A huge white bear ambling down the street was a sight to behold.

Exercise 7.3 | Convert the fragments below into whole sentences by rewriting or by combining them with the preceding or following words.

1. The king charged the bear's upkeep to the people of London. Who were already heavily taxed.

2. Henry decided to get a pet elephant. And to charge that to the people of London also.

3. When the elephant arrived, people flocked to see it. The first elephant in England.

_____

_____

4. Henry not the first English king to keep large pets.

_____

_____

5. William the Conqueror received a bear from his son William
   Rufus. As a gift. While another of William's sons reputedly had a
   large collection of his own.

_____

_____

6. Practically every crowned head feeling the desire to possess
   animals of great beauty or ferocity. Animals that were the biggest
   or the most dangerous. Or the most bizarre.

_____

_____

7. The Egyptian Queen Hatshepsut (1500 B.C.). She kept monkeys,
   leopards, and occasionally a giraffe. Within the palace grounds.
   Under the protection of the sun god.

_____

_____

8. Tiberius, who reigned in Rome from 12 to 37 A.D., kept an
   animal. His pet being a fairly large snake. Which he fed with his
   own hand. The snake becoming sick, after which it was dispatched
   by a colony of ants.

_____

_____

_____

9. Octavian, who became the Emperor Augustus, indulged his own passion for animals. By collecting talking birds.

_____

_____

_____

10. The Emperor Caracalla's unwillingness to leave home without taking his pet lions with him. And showing his affection for them by kissing them frequently.

_____

_____

_____

Recap

1. Avoid fragments by combining them with complete sentences.

   INCORRECT: The arctic is a hostile environment. Where frigid winds race across the ice.

   CORRECT: The arctic is a hostile environment where frigid winds race across the ice.

2. Convert fragments into complete sentences by adding or altering a verb.

   INCORRECT: The best type of stove being the "airtight" variety.

   CORRECT: The best type of stove _is_ the "airtight" variety.

   INCORRECT: Henry not the first English king to keep large pets.

   CORRECT: Henry _was_ not the first English king to keep large pets.

Posttest: Complete Sentences

Identify each group of words below as a complete sentence (OK) or as containing a fragment (F). Convert each fragment into a complete sentence or part of a complete sentence.

_____ 1. The Sierra "Haute Route" rarely has been travelled in winter.

_____

_____

_____ 2. Because of the obstacles of altitude and terrain that nature places in the path of the wilderness skier seeking to make this extraordinary crossing.

_____

_____

_____ 3. Thus far, only a few back-country skiers have made the attempt to cross the Sierra via this demanding route.

_____

_____

_____ 4. Their numbers are increasing. As stories about the visual and physical drama of the trip gain wider audiences.

_____

_____

_____ 5. The Sierra Haute Route being named appropriately after the famed traverse of the Swiss Alps.

_____

_____

_____ 6. This trans-Sierra crossing, a difficult challenge with its 13,000-foot passes.

_____

_____

_____ 7. It begins on the eastern edge of the Sierra, about 6 miles from the town of Independence. With its western terminus across the mountains at the Wolverton ranger station of Sequoia National Park.

_____

_____

_____ 8. Trying to cross the Sierra Nevada in winter by other routes, a challenge accepted by many skiers over the years.

_____

_____

_____ 9. A number of easier routes, like that across Yosemite's Tuolumne Meadows, where most of the terrain is relatively easy to cross.

_____

_____

_____ 10. But no other route reaching the heights of both altitude and visual impact of the Sierra Haute Route.

_____

_____

_____

Assignment

Proofread the following paragraph for fragments. (There are seven of them.) Then rewrite the paragraph, either converting the fragments into complete sentences or incorporating them as parts of other complete sentences.

The American artist Edward Hopper is sometimes called the painter of loneliness. Because his works often portray isolated individuals cut off from human contact. Hopper's loneliness, his detachment, not being the usual alienation from society shared by other artists. Other artists besides Hopper have felt alienated, that is, isolated and excluded from the society around them. However, for many artists, alienation, the sense of being an exile in one's own country, was something they could share with other artists. It being a form of companionship. But Hopper was different. Other alienated artists, at least since the nineteenth century, had been declaring their independence from the rules and limitations of society by revolting against the establishment. Their Bohemianism. Their eccentric behavior. In contrast, Hopper's alienation being a personal thing, inner and invisible, except in his art. Outwardly, he looked like a university professor. Content, for the most part, to wear for all occasions the convenient uniform of a good tweed jacket and slacks.

Chapter 8
Distinct Sentences

When a writer joins two complete sentences in a single sentence without any punctuation separating them or with only a comma separating them, the writer violates an important convention of Standard Written English. Stated very broadly, that convention requires that the boundary between distinct sentences be appropriately marked.

Two distinct sentences joined without any punctuation are sometimes called a *run-on sentence* or a *fused sentence.* One way in which these two distinct sentences can be punctuated correctly is by separating them with a period.

RUN-ON: Salamanders must maintain a moist skin they are frequently restricted to aquatic sites.

CORRECT: Salamanders must maintain a moist skin. They are frequently restricted to aquatic sites.

Two distinct sentences joined with a comma are sometimes called a *comma splice.* In the comma splice shown below, the comma can be replaced with a period, as in the earlier example. Another correct way to punctuate two distinct sentences like these is with a semicolon.

COMMA SPLICE: Salamanders must maintain a moist skin, they are frequently restricted to aquatic sites.

CORRECT: Salamanders must maintain a moist skin; they are frequently restricted to aquatic sites.

In the exercises that follow the Pretest, we will suggest these and other simple ways to convert comma splices and run-on sentences so that they conform to standard conventions.

Pretest: Distinct Sentences

Put the appropriate letter in the left-hand margin to identify comma splices (C) and run-ons (R), as well as complete sentences that are correctly punctuated (OK). Correct the errors you find by placing an appropriate punctuation mark above the place where the error occurs.

_____ 1. Salamanders are ectothermic (cold-blooded), their energetic needs are slight.

_____ 2. They need to feed infrequently, and they can remain inactive for long periods.

_____ 3. In many habitats, salamanders are the most abundant vertebrate, for example, salamanders in a New Hampshire forest were found to exceed birds and mammals in both numbers and biomass.

_____ 4. Salamanders display a variety of body shapes and sizes they range from inch-long species to an Asian genus whose members attain lengths of 5 feet.

_____ 5. Most species have well-developed legs and feet, others lack hind limbs entirely.

_____ 6. Some salamanders are fully aquatic, others are partly so, and many are fully terrestrial.

_____ 7. Some salamanders are subterranean others spend their lives far above the ground in the canopy of tropical forests.

_____ 8. Some salamanders capture insects and snails by partially flipping out a sticky tongue then they retrieve it with the prey attached.

_____ 9. In a fraction of a second, tropical salamanders can fire their tongues as far as a third of the length of their bodies; the long tongue makes it largely unnecessary for them to chase prey.

_____ 10. Many salamanders are adapted to life in trees, their webbed feet have evolved into suction cups, their tails can grasp stems and branches.

8a Separating Two Sentences with a Period or a Semicolon

We have rewritten a comma splice in two correct ways in the following example, first using a period and then a semicolon. (Chapter 13 says more about the semicolon.)

COMMA SPLICE: Morris, the world's best-known celebrity cat, works about twenty days a year, he earns $5000 to $10,000 for his work.

CORRECT: Morris, the world's best-known celebrity cat, works about twenty days a year. He earns $5000 to $10,000 for his work.

CORRECT: Morris, the world's best-known celebrity cat, works about twenty days a year; he earns $5000 to $10,000 for his work.

The next example shows a run-on sentence rewritten in two correct ways, first using a period and then a semicolon.

RUN-ON: Scientists have been unable to discover the secret of purring the apparatus and meaning of the cat's singular sound remain mysterious.

CORRECT: Scientists have been unable to discover the secret of purring. The apparatus and meaning of the cat's singular sound remain mysterious.

CORRECT: Scientists have been unable to discover the secret of purring; the apparatus and meaning of the cat's singular sound remain mysterious.

Exercise 8.1 | Using periods or semicolons, separate the comma splices and run-ons below into distinct sentences.

1. Some people believe humans domesticated the cat, others claim that Tabby decided to share life with us.

   _____

   _____

   _____

2. Cats may be biologically programmed for surviving in the wilderness training them may be impossible.

   _____

   _____

   _____

3. Many cat owners lavish elaborate care on their cats a few even take their pets to psychologists specializing in feline psyches.

   _____

   _____

   _____

4. Not all cats bask in luxury, some lead a hard life as strays.

_____

_____

_____

5. For the disturbed cat with a wealthy owner, there are a variety of animal practitioners, Dr. Michael Fox, a psychologist in Washington, D.C., advocates massage, both oriental and Swedish.

_____

_____

_____

8b Joining Two Sentences with a Coordinating Conjunction

Run-on sentences and comma splices can be converted into correctly joined sentences by using a comma and a *coordinating conjunction.* A coordinating conjunction is a word like *and, but, for, nor, or, so,* or *yet* that may join pairs of words, phrases, clauses, or sentences.

magazines <u>and</u> newspapers

in the air <u>or</u> on the ground

Marilyn's friends were late, <u>so</u> she read another chapter.

When it joins sentences, the conjunction should be preceded by a comma, which marks the boundary between the two sentences being joined.

In the next two examples, we first correct a run-on and then a comma splice by adding a comma and a conjunction.

RUN-ON: The first *Who's Who in America* appeared in 1899 its publisher readily admitted it was a copy of the *Who's Who* already published in England for half a century.

CORRECT: The first *Who's Who in America* appeared in 1899, <u>but</u> its publisher readily admitted it was a copy of the *Who's Who* already published in England for half a century.

COMMA SPLICE: No one needs to buy *Who's Who* to be in it, no one can buy a listing.

CORRECT: No one needs to buy *Who's Who* to be in it, <u>and</u> no one can buy a listing.

Exercise 8.2 | Using a comma and an appropriate coordinating conjunction, convert the comma splices and run-ons below into correctly joined sentences.

1. Albert Nelson Marquis should be a famous American, he was the founding publisher of *Who's Who in America.*

   _____

   _____

   _____

2. Marquis insisted that achievement was to be the criterion for listing, he refused to include the children or spouses of famous people unless they independently earned a place.

   _____

   _____

   _____

3. In America, athletes are surely among the most celebrated people they were not allowed in *Who's Who.*

   _____

   _____

   _____

4. Babe Ruth was never listed, his fame wasn't diminished.

   _____

   _____

   _____

5. Many show-business people were barred from the big red book Mae West was one of them.

   _____

   _____

   _____

6. Today Americans may be included in *Who's Who* based on the editors' evaluation of their achievement, they may be automatically admitted if they hold certain important jobs.

_____

_____

_____

7. Some famous people refuse to return a biography form to *Who's Who* others are excessively modest in their descriptions of themselves.

_____

_____

_____

8. Thomas Alva Edison was an impressive example of modesty, in the first volume of *Who's Who* he identified himself as an "electrician."

_____

_____

_____

9. Some of the reasons that determine who gets into *Who's Who* and who doesn't may be mysterious, the phrase "who's who" has become an idiom of the American language.

_____

_____

_____

10. Most of us have our own ideas of "who's who" we don't need to consult an authority.

_____

_____

_____

8c Joining Two Sentences with a Conjunctive Adverb

Comma splices and run-on sentences can be correctly rewritten using a semicolon or period followed by a *conjunctive adverb.*

Common Conjunctive Adverbs

accordingly	furthermore	namely
also	hence	nevertheless
anyhow	however	next
anyway	indeed	otherwise
besides	instead	still
consequently	likewise	then
finally	moreover	therefore

Conjunctive adverbs express relationships between complete sentences such as contrast, time, cause and effect, and conditions. In the following examples, a semicolon and a conjunctive adverb correct a comma splice and then a run-on sentence.

COMMA SPLICE: Small stereo tape-cassette players have become very popular, almost everyone seems to be walking around with headphones on.

CORRECT: Small, stereo tape-cassette players have become very popular; indeed, almost everyone seems to be walking around with headphones on.

RUN-ON: Sony was the first in the field with its *Walkman* a host of other audio manufacturers were quick to market similar walk-around players.

CORRECT: Sony was the first in the field with its *Walkman*; however, a host of other audio manufacturers were quick to market similar walk-around players.

In either example, a period could replace the semicolon preceding the conjunctive adverb, as illustrated here.

CORRECT: Sony was the first in the field with its *Walkman*. However, a host of other audio manufacturers were quick to market similar walk-around players.

Exercise 8.3 Using a semicolon and an appropriate conjunctive adverb, convert the comma splices and run-on sentences below into correctly joined sentences.

1. The cheapest headphone cassette players cost about $100 many people can afford them.

   _____

   _____

   _____

2. More expensive units may include additional features like FM radios, built-in loudspeakers, and recording capability, the simplest models are the most popular.

   _____

   _____

   _____

3. Tape players like the Sony *Walkman* are small they have the ability to reproduce sound of reasonably high fidelity.

   _____

   _____

   _____

4. The lightweight headphones can reproduce taped music at a very high volume, they do it without much distortion.

   _____

   _____

   _____

5. The whole idea of a walk-around tape player is portability smaller is better.

   _____

   _____

   _____

8d   Joining Two Sentences with a Subordinating Conjunction

Sometimes a comma splice or a run-on sentence can be correctly rewritten by means of a *subordinating conjunction.* Subordinating conjunctions express relationships between clauses such as time, place, manner, reason, contrast, and condition. A clause preceded by a subordinating conjunction is a dependent or subordinate clause. It cannot stand alone as a complete sentence.

> *Common Subordinating Conjunctions*
> *Time:* before, after, since, until, till, when, whenever, while, as
> *Place:* where, wherever
> *Manner:* as if, like
> *Reason:* because, since, as, so (that)
> *Contrast:* though, although, even though
> *Condition:* if, unless, whether (or not)

In the following examples, we have correctly rewritten a comma splice and then a run-on sentence by using subordinating conjunctions.

COMMA SPLICE: Fish make good pets, they don't bark or meow.

CORRECT: Fish make good pets <u>because</u> they don't bark or meow.

RUN-ON: Pet snails are easy to tell apart you simply paint their shells different colors.

CORRECT: Pet snails are easy to tell apart <u>if</u> you simply paint their shells different colors.

Exercise 8.4   Using an appropriate subordinating conjunction, convert the comma splices and run-on sentences below into single complete sentences.

1. Most people cannot afford to own airplanes, they are too expensive.

   _____

   _____

   _____

2. Would-be aviators who are handy with tools can build their own planes a fiberglass kit designed by Burt Rutan became available in 1976.

_____

_____

_____

3. The plane, called the VariEze, gets better gas mileage than most cars, it must be considered economical to fly.

_____

_____

_____

4. Not much room is required to construct the plane you will need at least the space of a two-car garage.

_____

_____

_____

5. You can build your own plane, you will need a license to fly it.

_____

_____

_____

8e Joining Two Sentences with a Relative Pronoun

Sometimes a *relative pronoun* may be used to convert the second sentence in a comma splice or run-on sentence into a particular kind of subordinate clause called a *relative clause*. Relative pronouns include *who, whom, whose, which,* and *that.* They connect a subordinate clause to a noun in another portion of the sentence.

> Edward Larrabee Barnes is the architect <u>who</u> designed the IBM Building in New York.

Who refers to *architect.* The clause, *who designed the IBM Building in New York,* is a relative clause. Relative clauses, which begin with a relative pronoun, provide information about the word referred to by the relative pronoun. In this case the relative pronoun specifies which architect the sentence it talking about.

In the next example, a comma splice is corrected by converting the second sentence into a relative clause.

COMMA SPLICE: The monarch butterfly is an amazing insect, it migrates more than 2000 miles to a winter refuge it has never seen.

CORRECT: The monarch butterfly is an amazing insect <u>that</u> migrates more than 2000 miles to a winter refuge it has never seen.

A run-on sentence may be corrected in a similar way.

RUN-ON: The body of a monarch butterfly contains magnetic material this may serve the insect as an internal compass.

CORRECT: The body of a monarch butterfly contains magnetic material <u>that</u> may serve the insect as an internal compass.

Exercise 8.5 | Use relative pronouns to convert the comma splices and run-on sentences below into single complete sentences.

1. Auto manufacturers are relying more and more on robots, they do not complain about unpleasant or dangerous work.

   _____

   _____

   _____

2. Robot welders can quickly and safely perform difficult tasks these were back-breaking for humans.

   _____

   _____

   _____

3. The Conrads are dedicated rose growers they lavish their time and attention on their plants.

   _____

   _____

   _____

4. One variety of yellow rose is named after Mrs. Conrad, her husband developed it by painstaking cross-fertilization.

_____

_____

_____

5. Mr. Conrad spent years experimenting with a thornless rose, unfortunately it lacked any scent.

_____

_____

_____

Recap

1. Separate distinct sentences with a period or a semicolon, but not with a comma.

RUN-ON: Cats may be biologically programmed for surviving in the wilderness training them may be impossible.

CORRECT: Cats may be biologically programmed for surviving in the wilderness. Training them may be impossible.

CORRECT: Cats may be biologically programmed for surviving in the wilderness; training them may be impossible.

COMMA SPLICE: Not all cats bask in luxury, some lead a hard life as strays.

CORRECT: Not all cats bask in luxury. Some lead a hard life as strays.

CORRECT: Not all cats bask in luxury; some lead a hard life as strays.

2. Join distinct sentences with a comma and a coordinating conjunction such as *and* or *but.*

COMMA SPLICE: Babe Ruth was never listed, his fame wasn't diminished.

CORRECT: Babe Ruth was never listed, but his fame wasn't diminished.

3. Join distinct sentences with a semicolon and a conjunctive adverb such as *however* or *nevertheless.*

RUN-ON: Sony was the first others quickly followed.

CORRECT: Sony was the first; however, others quickly followed.

4. Combine distinct sentences by using a subordinating conjunction such as *because* or *although.*

COMMA SPLICE: Most people cannot afford to own airplanes, they are too expensive.

CORRECT: Most people cannot afford to own airplanes because they are too expensive.

5. Combine distinct sentences by using a relative pronoun such as *who* or *which.*

RUN-ON: Burt Rutan designed the plane he calls it the VariEze.

CORRECT: Burt Rutan designed the plane, which he calls the VariEze.

Posttest: Distinct Sentences

In the left-hand margin, identify each group of words below as conventionally punctuated (OK), a comma splice (C), or a run-on sentence (R). Convert the comma splices and run-ons into conventionally punctuated sentences.

1. Some people don't believe music can be about anything, they say it doesn't have any subject matter.

_____

_____

_____

2. It is hard to think of a piece of music as having the same kind of subject matter as a painting or a novel music can't very easily refer to specific objects and events outside itself.

_____

_____

_____

———— 3. Some composers have tried to get around this limitation, and
          some of their attempts have almost succeeded.

          _____

          _____

          _____

———— 4. One method is to use sounds that imitate sounds that we hear in
          the world around us, Haydn used bird songs and clocks, Charles
          Ives used sirens.

          _____

          _____

          _____

———— 5. An accompanying narrative is another method of giving music
          content children love one work that does this, *Peter and the Wolf.*

          _____

          _____

          _____

———— 6. We depend on the words to tell the story we can't really say the
          music is about a boy and a wolf.

          _____

          _____

          _____

———— 7. Debussy wrote a work called *La Mer,* its title tells us that it's about
          the sea.

          _____

          _____

          _____

———— 8. The composer wanted his work to convey an impression of the sea
          its success in doing that depends on our knowing what he had in
          mind.

_____

_____   9. Debussy's work is beautiful, although it may not remind everyone of the ocean.

_____

_____   10. Part of the pleasure of music is the freedom it gives us, we can understand its "meaning" however we like.

_____

_____

Assignment

Proofread the following paragraph for comma splices, run-on sentences, and fragments. There are three of each. Then rewrite the paragraph using whole sentences that are conventionally punctuated.

The beach is not necessarily a pleasant environment. You sit on your blanket. Hoping for the best. A mob rushes onto the beach a helicopter thumps the air overhead. To your left, a gang of children is screaming. To your right, two dogs growling. The sky is full of inky, swirling clouds, huge waves crash onto the beach. A dozen transistor radios are blaring, each one is tuned to something different. Huge mounds of kelp are piled up on the shore the flies buzz endlessly past your ears. Some raucous teen-agers throwing a frisbee back and forth over your blanket. A man on a motorcycle whizzes past, his wheels spit sand in your face. You decide to leave then you discover your wallet is missing.

Chapter 9

Orderly Sentences

Clear sentences are orderly in the sense that they communicate by means of the order in which words, phrases, and clauses occur. Occasional problems arise when a writer uses an introductory phrase that doesn't fit with the words that follow it. What results can be unclear and illogical.

UNCLEAR: Dreaming about her vacation, the telephone surprised Mary.

The words "dreaming about her vacation" seem to be referring to *the telephone* instead of to *Mary.* Even though this order does not completely obscure its intended meaning, the sentence would be clearer and appear more logical if its introductory phrase were followed immediately by the word to which it refers, *Mary.*

CLEAR: Dreaming about her vacation, Mary jumped when the telephone rang.

A phrase, like *dreaming about her vacation,* that describes another word or phrase is called a *modifier* of that word or phrase. When a modifier is not immediately preceded or followed by the word or phrase it modifies, it is called a *dangling modifier* or a *misplaced modifier.*

Not only introductory phrases cause problems. Other misplaced modifiers may also create confusion or appear to be illogical. A misplaced modifier may make a sentence ambiguous, that is, allow it to be understood in more than one way.

UNCLEAR: Sarah promised her parents in June she would visit them.

Because of the position of the words *in June,* a reader cannot determine whether Sarah's promise was made in June or the visit is to take place in June. By moving *in June,* the writer can make either of these meanings clear.

CLEAR: Sarah promised her parents she would visit them in June.

CLEAR: In June Sarah promised her parents she would visit them.

Pretest: Orderly Sentences

In the left-hand margin, identify sentences with introductory dangling modifiers with a *D,* mark those that contain some other kind of misplaced modifier with an *M,* and indicate sentences with no such problems as *OK.* Revise sentences with dangling or misplaced modifiers so that they are clear and unambiguous.

_____ 1. Concerned with the rapidly increasing prices of fuel, wind power impresses a growing number of those who fish the West Coast commercially.

_____

_____

_____

_____ 2. Besides offering significant fuel savings, sails can enable the men and women who fish to get home safely in spite of an engine breakdown.

_____

_____

_____

_____ 3. One California fisherman, Dave Davies, built a steel-hulled fishing schooner, the *Cornucopia,* with both engine and sails near his home in Sacramento.

_____

_____

_____

_____ 4. Designed and built before the oil embargo sent fuel prices skyrocketing, each fishing trip to the area between Honolulu and the middle of the North Pacific now results in the boat saving Davies between two and three thousand dollars.

———— 5. Davies's son Morgan now builds schooners similar to the *Cornu-copia* for use in commercial fishing on a farm near Morro Bay, California.

9a   Avoiding Dangling Modifiers

Dangling modifiers often occur as introductory phrases that are not related to the words immediately following them. Sentences with dangling modifiers may confuse readers. Even more important, by appearing to be illogical, such sentences give an impression of carelessness and distract the reader's attention from what is being said.

UNCLEAR: In order to lose weight, the doctor advised John to give up chocolates.

The introductory phrase *in order to lose weight* seems to refer to *the doctor*, when in fact it refers to *John*. Rewording the sentence so that the introductory phrase follows *John* clarifies the meaning.

CLEAR: The doctor advised John to give up chocolates in order to lose weight.

Dangling modifiers cause problems because they are separated from the words they are meant to describe.

UNCLEAR: Careening down the slope, panic overwhelmed the novice skier.

The sentence above appears to say that panic was careening down the slope. The dangling phrase, *careening down the slope,* is separated from the words to which it was intended to refer, *the novice skier.* Rewording the sentence can make that connection clear and eliminate the apparent lack of logic.

CLEAR: Careening down the slope, the novice skier panicked.

Sometimes a dangling phrase occurs at the end of a sentence rather than at the beginning. The result is the same: the sentence may appear to be illogical.

UNCLEAR: Lately no food seems to please my cat served from a can.

The concluding phrase, *served from a can,* is a dangling construction. It seems to refer illogically to the words immediately preceding it, *my cat.* If the dangling phrase is placed directly after the word to which it actually refers, *food,* the problem disappears.

CLEAR: Lately no food served from a can seems to please my cat.

Exercise 9.1   Rewrite the sentences below to eliminate problems of clarity and logic caused by dangling constructions.

1. To explain the origins of the Christmas tree, Martin Luther is the subject of a story.

   _____

   _____

   _____

2. Walking through the countryside one winter night, some say Luther first got the idea for the Christmas tree.

   _____

   _____

   _____

3. Spellbound by the scent of fir trees and the twinkling of bright stars overhead, an inspiration struck Luther.

   _____

   _____

   _____

4. To share some of his joy and wonder at the beauty of creation, a fir tree was brought by Luther into his family quarters in the old Augustinian monastery at Wittenberg.

   _____

   _____

   _____

5. Luther's children were surprised and delighted when they saw the tree set up by their father decorated with candles.

   _____

   _____

   _____

9b Avoiding Misplaced Modifiers

A misplaced modifier can occur anywhere in a sentence, making it unclear or ambiguous.

UNCLEAR: Our football coach spoke about how to win games on television.

The words *on television* seem to refer to *games.* But the writer intended to say that the coach appeared on television to talk about how to win games—all games, not just televised ones. Clarity requires that the misplaced modifier, *on television,* be placed closer to the word it modifies, *spoke.*

CLEAR: Our football coach spoke on television about how to win games.

Now the meaning of the sentence is unambiguous.

Placing modifiers close to the words they refer to usually results in clarity, but not always.

UNCLEAR: Anyone who teases rattlesnakes very often regrets it.

Is the phrase *very often* a modifier of *teases rattlesnakes* or of *regrets it*? The meaning of this sentence is unclear because *very often* is adjacent to both phrases, each of which it might modify. The writer might have meant to refer to people who often tease rattlesnakes or to say that people very often regret teasing rattlesnakes.

CLEAR: Anyone who very often teases rattlesnakes regrets it.

CLEAR: Anyone who teases rattlesnakes regrets it very often.

Moving *very often* in front of *teases* gives the sentence one clear meaning; moving *very often* to the end of the sentence results in another clear meaning.

Exercise 9.2 | Rewrite the sentences below to eliminate problems of ambiguity caused by misplaced modifiers.

1. For many centuries fireworks have thrilled people against the nighttime sky.

   _____

   _____

   _____

2. Various researchers into pyrotechnic history give credit to Arabic, Greek, German, Chinese, and Indian inventors, although they admit they are speculating.

   _____

   _____

   _____

3. Military engineers who used gunpowder for destruction routinely employed it to entertain as well.

   _____

   _____

   _____

4. During and after the Renaissance, European courts put on fireworks displays splendidly celebrating coronations, marriages, victories, treaties, and religious festivals.

   _____

   _____

   _____

5. Music was often included in these fiery performances. The *Royal Fireworks* suite that Handel composed beautifully accompanied fireworks in 1749.

_____

_____

_____

Recap

1. A dangling modifier occurs when an introductory or concluding phrase seems to be attached to words that it does not really describe. Rewrite sentences with dangling modifiers by placing the dangling phrase directly before or after the phrase it modifies.

   UNCLEAR: Dreaming about her vacation, the telephone surprised Mary.

   CLEAR: Dreaming about her vacation, Mary jumped when the telephone rang.

2. A misplaced modifier is a word or phrase that because of its position, is not clearly connected to the words it modifies. Rewrite sentences with misplaced modifiers by moving the modifier to a position in which its meaning is clear.

   UNCLEAR: Sarah promised her parents in June she would visit them.

   CLEAR: Sarah promised her parents she would visit them in June.

   CLEAR: In June Sarah promised her parents she would visit them.

Posttest: Orderly Sentences

Some of the sentences below are illogical or unclear because of dangling constructions or misplaced modifiers. Rewrite such sentences to eliminate the problem. Identify sentences that you find acceptable by writing *OK* after them.

1. Learning that I was about to move from Los Angeles to Minneapolis, my motives were questioned by my friends.

   _____

   _____

   _____

2. Colette had heard that Minneapolis has an average winter low temperature of 4 degrees and an annual snowfall of 42 inches on television.

   _____

   _____

   _____

3. Harvey extended his arms straight out repeatedly exclaiming, "Snow that deep! Snow that deep!"

   _____

   _____

   _____

4. After listening to them for a while, I finally managed to get them to stop and listen to me.

   _____

   _____

   _____

5. Having understood my admiration for Minneapolis as a cultural center, my decision was accepted by Colette.

   _____

   _____

   _____

6. None of my examples of fine theatres, art galleries, and museums satisfied Harvey, determined as he was to disapprove of my decision.

_____

_____

_____

7. He refused even to consider my reasons, being very stubborn.

_____

_____

_____

8. My descriptions of friendly neighborhoods, quaint shops, and lively coffee houses were also ineffective until I remembered that in personal matters arguing with Harvey logically makes him mad.

_____

_____

_____

9. Having known Harvey for a long time, his hurt feelings over my sudden move to Minneapolis should really not have surprised me.

_____

_____

_____

10. The next morning, stuffed in my mailbox, I found Harvey's note of apology.

_____

_____

_____

Assignment

Proofread the following paragraph for dangling constructions and misplaced modifiers. Then rewrite the five sentences needing revision.

A railroad runs three times each day through the jungle between Bangkok and Nam Tok in Thailand, built at a cost of thousands of human lives. The tracks are part of what was once called the Death Railroad. Constructed by slave laborers and prisoners of war, the Japanese Imperial Army Command was provided with a vital land route from Singapore and Bangkok to Burma by the railroad. For nearly thirty years now, British, Australian, and Dutch tour groups traveling in Asia regularly have made this railroad part of a pilgrimage destination. In the city of Kanchanaburi, about halfway between Bangkok and Nam Tok, a small museum is maintained by Buddhist monks documenting the suffering of those who built the railroad. Stepping into the sunlight after a deeply moving visit to the museum, gratitude is felt by the visitor as a monk bows to him with a gesture that seems to say, "Remember, but forgive."

Chapter 10

Subject/Verb Agreement

The convention that subjects and verbs must "agree" is easy to follow most of the time if the patterns of your spoken dialect happen to coincide with those of Standard Written English. Then, for example, you would quite automatically choose the first and not the second of the following two examples.

CORRECT: The <u>dancers</u> <u>were</u> spinning gracefully around the room.

INCORRECT: The <u>dancers</u> <u>was</u> spinning gracefully around the room.

In grammatical terms, we would say that when the subject is plural (more than one), then the verb must be plural also. *Dancers* requires *were*, not *was*. If the subject is singular, then the verb must be singular as well, as in the following example.

CORRECT: The *dancer was* spinning gracefully around the room.

Difficulty with this convention usually occurs when, for some reason, it is not easy to determine whether the subject is singular or plural, as in the following example.

Each of the dancers (spin/spins) gracefully.

Each is the subject, not *dancers*. Since *each* is singular, the verb must be the singular *spins*, not the plural *spin*. In the exercises that follow the Pretest, we will give you practice in solving the most frequent problems of agreement between subject and verb.

Pretest: Subject/Verb Agreement

Write in the form of the verb that agrees with the subject of the sentence.

1. The master builders of the great Gothic cathedrals like Notre Dame (was/were) _____ for the most part illiterate.

2. Building those soaring structures (seems/seem) _____ amazing to us even today.

3. However, most of the historians who study that period (believes/believe) _____ that those medieval artisans could neither read, write, nor multiply.

4. Notre Dame, like the other great cathedrals, (depends/depend) _____ on flying buttresses to support its magnificent vaults.

5. These slender arches of stone (transfers/transfer) _____ the enormous horizontal thrust of the cathedral vaults to weight-bearing vertical piers—tall stacks of stone blocks.

6. Each of the great cathedrals (relies/rely) _____ on this brilliant engineering discovery of the Middle Ages.

7. There (is/are) _____ several other key elements of Gothic style besides the flying buttress, including ribbed vaulting and the pointed arch.

8. All three features (contributes/contribute) _____ to the beauty of the cathedral.

9. But aesthetics alone (does/do) _____ not explain these trademarks of Gothic style; each of them (seems/seem) _____ to play a structural role as well.

10. Nevertheless, each of the visitors to Notre Dame or Chartres (takes/take) _____ away an impression of spiritual power, not just clever engineering.

10a   Agreement of Separated Subject and Verb

It's often hard to determine whether a verb should be singular or plural when intervening words separate the verb from its subject.

A moose whose young calf is attacked by wolves (<u>defends</u>/defend) her off-spring with ferocity.

A moose is the subject. Because this subject is singular, *defends* is the form of the verb that agrees with it.

10b   Agreement of Compound Subject and Verb

A compound subject contains two or more subjects joined by *and* or *or*. Two singular subjects joined by *and* (or *both . . . and*) agree with a plural verb.

A mother and her calf (shares/<u>share</u>) a close bond.

An exception to this pattern occurs when the singular subjects joined by *and* are preceded by *each* or *every*. Then a singular verb is required.

Each mother and each calf (<u>faces</u>/face) the danger of attack by predators.

Singular subjects joined by *or* (or by *either . . . or* or *neither . . . nor*) agree with a singular verb.

A wolf or a bear (<u>is</u>/are) a threat to an undefended calf.

When a singular subject and a plural subject are joined by *or* (or by *either . . . or,* or *neither . . . nor*), the verb agrees with the subject nearer to it.

Either drowning or chill winds (is/<u>are</u>) a danger for calves who escape predators.

Exercise 10.1 | In the sentences below, write in the verb form that agrees with the subject.

1. Neither of the calves born to the young mother moose (appears/appear) _____ to be undernourished.

2. A mother accompanied by newborn calves (chases/chase) _____ away her calves born the previous year.

3. Three wolves and a grizzly bear (follows/follow) _____ the herd of grazing moose.

4. Thirteen adult moose, but not a single calf, (was/were) _____ observed at the ranger station.

5. If wolves or a bear (happens/happen) _____ to come upon a bull moose exhausted from battling with other bulls, a kill becomes very likely.

6. The extreme cold and the deep snows (poses/pose) _____ a challenge to all moose in the Mt. McKinley region.

7. One clear principle illustrated by the life of the Alaskan moose (is/are) _____ that only the fittest survive.

8. As a result, the ones a summer back-packer sees grazing in the meadows (looks/look) _____ strong and healthy.

9. The forces of nature (acts/act) _____ to keep all the elements of the subarctic ecosystem in balance.

10. Large numbers of humans in recreational vehicles, a new element in the delicate subarctic, (threatens/threaten) _____ this balance.

10c   Agreement of Verbs and Special Noun Constructions

10c(1)   Plural Nouns with Singular Meanings

Some nouns, like *measles* and *economics,* are plural in form, but when their meanings are singular, they agree with a singular verb, as in the following examples.

> Measles <u>is</u> sometimes a serious illness.
>
> Home economics <u>describes</u> what every liberated man needs to know.

In addition to *measles* and *economics,* verbs are usually singular with subjects like these: *aesthetics, checkers, mathematics, mumps, physics, politics, statistics.* However, occasionally some of these words occur with plural meanings, and then they agree with a plural verb. For example, when *checkers* refers to the game, it is singular.

Checkers <u>is</u> a popular game.

When *checkers* refers to the individual pieces used in playing the game, it is plural.

Three checkers <u>are</u> missing from the game box.

10c(2)   Indefinite Pronouns

Indefinite pronouns do not refer to particular persons or things. Some indefinite pronouns, like *everyone,* always require singular verbs.

Everyone <u>knows</u> that mistakes are possible.

Indefinite pronouns like *everyone* seem to refer to a number of people, when actually they refer to only one. Verbs are always singular with these indefinite pronouns: *each, either, neither, one, everyone, everybody, no one, nobody, anyone, anybody, someone,* or *somebody.*

A subject like *some* or *most* may require a singular or a plural verb, depending on how it is understood in the context of the words that accompany it.

Most of the bread <u>is</u> baked.

Most of the bills <u>are</u> paid.

In the first example, *most* has a singular meaning; in the second example, *most* is understood as plural. Verbs may be singular or plural with the following subjects, depending on their meaning and context: *all, any, more, most, none, some.*

10c(3)   Collective Nouns

A singular or a plural verb may agree with such *collective nouns* as *committee, crew, group, majority, number,* and *team,* depending on whether they are understood as referring to a group as a single unit or as a collection of individuals or things.

The number of votes cast in the election <u>was</u> huge.

A number of ballots <u>were</u> illegible.

When the group is understood as a single entity, use a singular verb.

The basketball team <u>holds</u> its practice sessions in the gym.

When the members of the group are being referred to individually, use a plural verb.

The sales team <u>disagree</u> among themselves about their manager's decision.

Exercise 10.2 | In the sentences below, write in the verb form that agrees with the subject.

1. Politics (plays/play) _____ a role in the selection of Academy Award winners.

2. Most of the films that win (is/are) _____ promoted with great publicity.

3. Each of the stars nominated (hopes/hope) _____ to win the coveted statue.

4. A majority of the judges (seems/seem) _____ to cast their votes in favor of mediocrity.

5. A majority of the audience (is/are) _____ apparently willing to spend its leisure time and extra money viewing films that exploit violence and sex.

6. Everyone who (pays/pay) _____ to see those films (encourages/encourage) _____ Hollywood to produce more of them.

7. Most of the serious film criticism in newspapers and magazines (seems/seem) _____ to agree about the need for improvement.

8. None of the major studios (dares/dare) _____ to take a risk by changing a very profitable formula.

9. Probably a group of greedy investors (finances/finance) _____ only those films that it believes will make a lot of money.

10. To make matters worse, in most theatres neither the popcorn nor the other snacks (tastes/taste) _____ very good.

10d   Agreement of Reversed Subject and Verb

A verb and its subject agree even when the subject follows the verb.

Blowing in the air (was/<u>were</u>) great clouds of dust.

The plural verb *were* agrees with the plural subject *clouds.*
    Frequently the subject follows the verb in sentences beginning with the word *there.*

There (is/<u>are</u>) many reasons for the problem.

The plural verb *are* agrees with the plural subject *reasons.*

There (has/<u>have</u>) been increases in erosion.

The plural verb *have* agrees with the plural subject *increases.*

Exercise 10.3   In the sentences below, write in the verb form that agrees with the subject.

1. In the Dust Bowl days of the 1930s, there (was/were) _____ terrible difficulties with soil erosion.

2. Only recently (has/have) _____ the dangers of soil erosion once again become a major concern for farmers.

3. Throughout America (is/are) _____ farmers who have ignored conservation practices.

4. Chief among the reasons for bad soil-conservation practices (has/have) _____ been the desire among farmers to use gigantic modern farm machinery efficiently.

5. As a result, in some parts of the country there (remains/remain) _____ very few of the old terraces and windbreaks that for many years retarded erosion.

Recap

1. Verbs agree with subjects even when they are separated by other words.

   A moose whose young calf is attacked by wolves defends her offspring with ferocity.

2. A plural verb agrees with singular subjects joined by *and.*

   A mother and her calf share a close bond.

3. A singular verb agrees with singular subjects joined by *or.*

   A wolf or a bear is a threat to a newborn calf.

4. When a singular and a plural subject are joined by *or,* the verb agrees with the subject nearer to it.

   If wolves or a bear attacks an undefended calf, a kill is likely.

5. Verbs are usually singular with nouns that are plural in form but singular in meaning, such as *mathematics* and *politics.*

   Politics is not for everyone.

6. Verbs are singular with indefinite pronouns, such as *each* and *anyone.*

   Anyone knows the answer to that question.

7. Verbs may be singular or plural with subjects like *all, most,* and *some.*

   Most of the bread is baked.

   Most of the bills are paid.

8. A singular or a plural verb may agree with collective nouns such as *committee* and *team.*

   The committee meets each week.

   The committee disagree with each other about the measure.

9. A verb and subject agree even when the subject follows the verb.

   Over the windows hangs an awning.

Posttest: Subject/Verb Agreement

In the sentences below, write in the form of the verb that agrees with the subject.

1. Almost everyone in American literature classes (imagines/imagine) _____ Walt Whitman as an elderly, bearded man.

2. But the study of his life and writings (reveals/reveal) _____ the younger Whitman as an equally fascinating character.

3. Neither his school teaching nor his work on newspapers really (explains/explain) _____ how he came to write *Leaves of Grass.*

4. Again and again in his poems (recurs/recur) _____ the themes of faith in democracy and trust in the individual.

5. A number of his poems (expresses/express) _____ his response to the horrors of the Civil War.

6. The courage of the sick and dying men and boys (was/were)

_____ an inspiration to Whitman in his work as an unoffi-

cial nurse in military hospitals.

7. One of Whitman's most loved poems (describes/describe) _____

his grief and consolation at the death of President Lincoln.

8. There (is/are) _____ few American poems more widely

admired than "When Lilacs Last in the Dooryard Bloom'd."

9. Whitman's vision of America and his hope for its future

(continues/continue) _____ to inspire his readers today.

10. Not one of America's other poets (has/have) _____ been

able to express the national spirit more movingly.

Assignment

Proofread the following paragraph for errors in agreement of subject and
verb. There are eight of them. Correct each agreement error.

One widespread and extremely persistent myth is that English
teachers is the arbiters of language. Everyone who once attended
elementary school recall being drilled in the rules of "good"
English. There seems to have been one or two teachers in everyone's past who confirms the stereotype of the fussy corrector of
mistakes. However, not one of the real standards of usage depend
for validity on English teachers or grammarians. Neither the
English teacher nor the grammarian create the rules. In reality,
each of these "authorities" are needed only to observe objectively
the language patterns and practices of educated people and to
teach these patterns to any of us who want to communicate in an
educated way. The judgmental English teacher in most people's
fantasies do not really correspond to the likable people who are
teaching the art and craft of writing today.

Chapter 11

Pronoun Choice

A pronoun almost always refers to a noun or pronoun (its *antecedent*) that occurs near it, and it is conventional in Standard Written English that the form of the pronoun used agree in specific ways with the antecedent. If the noun referred to is singular, for example, then the pronoun must also be singular (the woman . . . <u>she</u>). If the noun is plural, then the pronoun must also be plural (the women . . . <u>they</u>).

The bees returned to <u>their</u> hives.

Every bee had accomplished <u>its</u> task.

Their is plural in agreement with *bees*. *Its* is singular in agreement with *bee*.

Feminine pronouns refer to feminine nouns (Carol . . . *she*), and masculine pronouns refer to masculine nouns (uncle . . . *his*).

Carol visited <u>her</u> uncle.

Carol's uncle lost <u>his</u> pipe.

The plural pronoun *their* can refer to the plural of masculine, feminine, or neuter nouns.

The women raised <u>their</u> hands.

The men raised <u>their</u> hands.

The trees dropped <u>their</u> leaves.

Furthermore, conventional usage requires that specific forms of some pronouns be used according to their grammatical function in the sentence.

Mayor Brown and <u>she</u> met for an hour.

Because it functions as part of the subject, *she* is the correct form, not *her.*

The mayor then scheduled a second appointment with <u>her</u>.

Her is the correct form for the object of the preposition *with.*

In the exercises following the Pretest, we will give you practice with some of the most important conventions for the use of pronouns.

Pretest: Pronoun Choice

Write in the correct pronoun form in the sentences below.

1. Climbing great mountains can have great dangers associated with (it/them) _____ .

2. The Eiger in Switzerland or Everest in Nepal cannot be taken lightly even by (its/their) _____ most experienced climbers.

3. Overcoming either peak will require facing (its/their) _____ particular hazards.

4. Before 1858, not one of the climbers (who/which) _____ challenged the Eiger completed (his/their) _____ trip.

5. The north face and the west flank of the Eiger present different degrees of challenge to (its/their) _____ climbers.

6. My friend Andrea and (I/me) _____ planned to climb the Eiger's dangerous north face with the help of a guide named Fritz.

7. After flying to Zurich, I met Andrea and (he/him) _____ in Grindelwald, at the mountain's foot.

8. Fritz asked both of us to summarize (her/our) _____ previous climbing experience.

9. Fritz questioned Andrea and (I/me) _____ for a short

time.

10. Then he declared that (she and I/her and I) _____ would

probably be sufficiently challenged by an afternoon stroll in the

woods.

11a   Agreement of Pronouns and Compound Antecedents

11a(1)   Nouns Joined by *And*

When a pronoun refers to two nouns joined by *and* (or *both . . . and*), the
pronoun should be plural.

> Watson and Nicklaus picked up their golf clubs.
>
> Both the caddy and the greens keeper expressed their surprise.

11a(2)   Nouns Preceded by *Each* or *Every*

An exception to the preceding pattern occurs when the nouns follow *each*
or *every;* then the pronoun should be singular.

> Each golfer and each caddy expressed his appreciation.

The pronoun *his* in this case refers to *each golfer* and *each caddy* separately.
His is correct if all the golfers and caddies are male. If they are all female,
her is the correct form.

> Each golfer and each caddy expressed her appreciation.

If the golfers and caddies are a mixed group of men and women, they may
be referred to by *his or her.*

> Each golfer and each caddy expressed his or her appreciation.

An alternative to using *his or her* is to revise the sentence, making the nouns
plural. Then the pronoun referring to the group is the plural *their.*

> All the golfers and caddies expressed their appreciation.

11a(3) Nouns Joined by *Or*

Pronouns that refer to singular nouns joined by *or* (or by *either . . . or,* or *neither . . . nor*) should be singular.

Either Watson or Nicklaus struck <u>his</u> club on a rock.

Exercise 11.1 Write in the correct pronoun form in the sentences below. Underline the word or words that the pronoun refers to.

1. In the 1977 British Open Golf Tournament in Turnberry, Watson and Nicklaus were tied for first after (his/their) _____ first thirty-six holes.

2. Each golfer shot a 65 in (his/their) _____ third round.

3. Neither Watson nor Nicklaus played less than (his/their) _____ best.

4. Every one of us watching held (his or her/our) _____ breath during the last round, when Watson shot another 65 to edge Nicklaus by one stroke.

5. Both Mrs. Kilgallan and Mrs. Peabody followed every shot with (her/their) _____ binoculars that year, in which the game of golf saw one of (his or her/its) _____ finest matches.

11b Agreement of Pronouns and Special Noun Constructions

11b(1) Plural Nouns with Singular Meanings

Some nouns, like *mathematics* and *politics,* are plural in form, but when their meanings are singular, pronouns referring to them should also be singular.

Mathematics is an ancient discipline; <u>it</u> provides the foundation for modern science.

Politics demands a great deal of <u>its</u> practitioners.

Pronouns referring to the following nouns are usually singular: *aesthetics, checkers, economics, mathematics, measles, mumps, physics, politics.*

11b(2)   Indefinite Pronouns

A pronoun referring to some indefinite pronouns, like *everyone,* should be singular.

Everyone presented his ideas for the project.

Everyone presented her ideas for the project.

NOT: Everyone presented their ideas . . .

Words like *everyone* seem to refer to a number of people, when actually they refer to only one. Pronouns are always singular when they refer to these indefinite pronouns: *each, either, neither, one, everyone, everybody, no one, nobody, anyone, anybody, someone, somebody.*

Indefinite pronouns like *anyone* and *everyone* are neither masculine nor feminine. As a result, writers may solve the problem of agreement by using *his or her* and *he or she.*

Everyone on the committee expressed his or her opinion.

An alternative to using this construction is to rewrite the sentence using plurals.

All the members of the committee expressed their opinions.

Either a singular or a plural pronoun may agree with indefinite pronouns like *some* or *most,* depending on whether the indefinite pronoun refers to a singular or a plural noun.

Some of the money is not in its usual place.

Some of the books are not in their usual places.

Pronouns may be singular or plural when they refer to the following indefinite pronouns, depending on context: *all, any, more, most, none, some.*

11b(3) Collective Nouns

A singular or a plural pronoun may agree with such collective nouns as *committee, crew, group, majority, number,* and *team,* depending on whether they refer to a group as a single unit or as a collection of individuals or things.

> The committee held *its* first public meeting.
>
> The committee disagreed among *themselves* about *their* meeting time.

Exercise 11.2 | In the sentences below, write in the correct pronoun form. Underline the word or words with which the pronoun agrees.

1. Anyone who visits Michigan's Mackinac Island must leave (his or her/their) _____ car on the mainland.

2. Visitors and residents alike must either walk or use a bicycle or horse-drawn carriage as (his or her/their) _____ means of transportation on the picturesque island.

3. Most of the permanent population depends on tourism for (its/their) _____ income.

4. Almost none of the island's 750,000 annual visitors can leave without taking (his or her/their) _____ mandatory taste or two of the island's famous fudge.

5. Caring for Mackinac's 600 horses, however, is not without (its/their) _____ problems. Residents of "Horse and Buggy Island" get (his or her/their) _____ share of fly bites during the summer season.

11c Case

11c(1) Subjective Case

The pronoun forms *I, we, you, he, she, it,* and *they* function grammatically as subjects. These forms are called *subjective case* forms.

John and I saw the same film.

NOT: John and me saw the same film.

Cynthia and he had read the book.

NOT: Cynthia and him had read the book.

In these examples *I* and *he* are the correct forms because each is part of the grammatical subject of its sentence.

This convention is usually troublesome only in the case of plural subjects like "John and I." Hardly anyone is likely to say "Him had read the book," or "Me saw the film." When you are not sure which pronoun form to use in a plural subject ("Cynthia and he/him had read . . ."), try out your sentence with the pronoun alone as subject ("He/Him had read . . .").

The same pronoun forms that serve as subjects are also correct when they serve as *predicate nominatives,* the grammatical function of nouns and pronouns that follow a form of the verb *be* when *be* means "equals."

Bill's best friends are John and I.

NOT: . . . are John and me.

This sentence means "Bill's best friends = John and I."

The first guests to arrive were Susan and he.

NOT: . . . were Susan and him.

11c(2)   Objective Case

The pronoun forms *me, us, you, him, her, it,* and *them* are in the *objective case* and function grammatically as *direct objects, indirect objects,* and *objects of prepositions.*

Direct objects follow verbs and receive the action of the verb.

Gerald wrecked his car.

To identify the direct object, ask *who* or *what* after the subject or verb. For example, Gerald wrecked what? He wrecked his car. *Car* is thereby identified as the direct object.

Use objective case pronouns as direct objects.

The principal phoned the Smiths and us.

NOT: . . . phoned the Smiths and we.

Falling plaster struck both Sally and <u>her</u>.

NOT: . . . struck both Sally and <u>she</u>.

An indirect object is the person or thing for whom or to whom the action is done. Indirect objects usually occur together with direct objects.

Aunt Mary sent <u>John</u> a sweater.

To whom did Aunt Mary send a sweater? She sent it to *John*—the indirect object.

Use objective case pronouns as indirect objects.

General Telephone refunded my wife and <u>me</u> the money.

NOT: . . . refunded my wife and <u>I</u> the money.

That teacher gave the other class and <u>us</u> low grades.

NOT: . . . gave the other class and <u>we</u> low grades.

A noun or pronoun that follows a preposition (such as *at, on, in, over, under, from,* or *with*) is called the object of the preposition. Use objective case pronouns after prepositions.

To the other members and <u>me</u>, that policy seems wrong.

NOT: To the other members and <u>I</u> . . .

The girls with Joan and <u>him</u> are their nieces.

NOT: . . . with Joan and <u>he</u> . . .

Again, problems are more likely to occur when the pronoun form is part of a plural object. Probably no one would say or write "To <u>I</u> that policy seems wrong," or "Falling plaster struck <u>she</u>." When you are not sure about the correct form of a pronoun in a compound object (". . . struck both Sally and <u>her</u>"), test the pronoun in the phrase by itself ("struck <u>her</u>").

Sometimes it is difficult to choose the correct pronoun form following the comparative words *as* and *than*. The correct form is determined by the grammatical function of the pronoun in a part of the sentence that is unstated and must be understood from context.

Weber wrote a longer essay than <u>I</u> [wrote].

NOT: . . . than <u>me</u>.

I, however, argued more convincingly than he [argued].

NOT: . . . than him.

In the examples, the words understood from context are in brackets. *I* and *he* are correct because each functions as the subject of the unstated part of the sentence.

A pronoun following *as* or *than* may also serve as an object in the unstated part of the sentence.

That novel puzzled the teacher as much as [it puzzled] us.

OR: That novel puzzled the teacher as much as we [puzzled the teacher].

Your boss pays you the same as [he pays] her.

OR: Your boss pays you the same as she [pays you].

Us and *her* function as direct objects in the unstated portions of the sentences. *We* and *she* function as subjects.

Like is a preposition. A pronoun following *like* serves as its object.

A beautiful movie star like her probably has many boyfriends.

Carl, like me, is over six feet tall.

11c(3) *Who and Whom*

Use *who* as subject; use *whom* as object.

I sold my calculator to the student who sat next to me. (*Who* is the subject of *sat*).

Terry pointed at the man whom he had talked to. (*Whom* is the object of *to*.)

It may help you decide between *who* and *whom* to try rephrasing the troublesome construction as a simple sentence, replacing the *who/whom* that you are unsure about with *he* or *him*. Where *he* fits, *who* is the correct form. Where *him* fits, *whom* is correct.

_____ did the IRS call in for an audit?
(Who or whom?)

The IRS called him in (not he). Therefore, the correct form is

<u>Whom</u> did the IRS call in for an audit?

In the next example, we would say that we believe <u>he</u> discovered gunpowder (not <u>him</u>).

_____ do we believe discovered gunpowder?
(*Who or whom?*)

<u>Who</u> do we believe discovered gunpowder?

In the last example, you would say to yourself, "I have learned from <u>him</u>" (not <u>he</u>).

I always recommend a teacher _____ I have learned from.
(*Who or whom?*)

I always recommend a teacher <u>whom</u> I have learned from.

Whom is the object of *from,* even though *whom* does not directly follow *from.*

Exercise 11.3 | Write in the correct pronoun form in the sentences below.

1. Most of (we/us) _____ have never heard of James Bonsack, the inventor of the automatic cigarette rolling machine.

2. After the twenty-year-old Bonsack filed for a patent on his invention in 1880, success came quickly for his father and (he/him) _____ .

3. The elder Bonsack and (he/him) _____ set up a company to manufacture the machines, and soon cheap, factory-made cigarettes were abundant.

4. A slightly earlier development during the 1870s had set the stage for their company and (they/them) _____ .

5. The discovery of a new way of processing tobacco leaves provided the Bonsacks and (we/us) _____ with a pleasurable way to addict ourselves to nicotine.

6. Older cigarettes had tasted harsh; the new cigarettes, much milder than (they/them) _____ , tasted good.

7. The popularity of cigarette smoking grew quickly among Americans in the last third of the nineteenth century. No one appreciated cheap, good-tasting cigarettes more than (they/them) _____ .

8. Happy cigarette manufacturers were getting rich quickly, and their new product seemed to please their customers as much as (they/them) _____ .

9. Our parents and grandparents, (who/whom) _____ we know grew up with less awareness of the hazards of smoking than (we/us), _____ may have smoked enthusiastically.

10. But for today's smokers like you and (I/me) _____ , who know that inhaled cigarette smoke can be lethal, little pleasure remains in the deadly habit.

Recap

1. Singular pronouns agree with singular nouns, and plural pronouns with plural nouns.

    Every bee accomplished its task.

    The bees returned to their hives.

2. Plural pronouns agree with nouns joined by *and.*

    Watson and Nicklaus picked up their clubs.

3. Singular pronouns agree with nouns joined by *or.*

    Either Watson or Nicklaus broke his club.

4. Singular pronouns agree with some plural nouns that have singular meanings.

Politics demands much from its practitioners.

5. Singular pronouns agree with indefinites like *everyone* and *nobody.*

    Everyone presented his ideas for the project.

    Everyone presented her ideas for the project.

    Everyone presented his or her ideas for the project.

6. Either a singular or a plural pronoun may agree with some indefinite pronouns, depending on whether they refer to a singular or a plural noun.

    Some of the money is not in its usual place.

    Some of the books are not in their usual places.

7. Subject forms of pronouns function as subjects and predicate nominatives.

    John and I saw the film.

    Bill's best friends are John and I.

8. Object forms of pronouns function as direct and indirect objects and as objects of prepositions.

    The principal phoned the Smiths and us.

    People like Joan and him value privacy.

9. After *as* and *than*, the pronoun form depends on unstated words understood from context.

    Weber wrote a longer essay than I [wrote].

    It puzzled the teacher as much as [it puzzled] us.

10. Use *who* as subject; use *whom* as object.

    The officer who arrived first gave Dick a ticket.

    Four classmates whom we invited couldn't come.

Posttest: Pronoun Choice

Write in the correct pronoun forms in the sentences below.

1. Scientists from the University of Washington constantly monitor Mount St. Helens with (his/their) _____ instruments.

2. They seek data that will help other researchers and (they/them) _____ put together a clearer picture of the earth's interior.

3. Anyone who studies volcanoes may be putting (himself/themselves) _____ in danger.

4. In May of 1980, the eruption of Mount St. Helens took the lives of several persons. Among (they/them) _____ was the young vulcanologist David Johnston.

5. Although his colleagues and (he/him) _____ expected an eventual eruption, no one making research trips to the volcano believed it would explode while (he/they) _____ was actually on or near it.

6. Just like you and (I/me) _____ , scientists were awestruck by that display of the earth's inner power.

7. Modern geophysics relates eruptions of volcanoes like Mount St. Helens to (its/their) _____ theory of continental drift.

8. Early in this century the German scientist Alfred Wegener first proposed that the continents actually move over the surface of the earth. Perhaps no scientist since Galileo met with more skepticism than (he/him) _____ .

9. Today referred to as "global plate tectonics," Wegener's view of the earth's surface as a mobile jigsaw puzzle fascinates scientists as much as it does (we/us) _____ laypeople.

10. People like (we/us) _____ Californians, (who/whom)

_____ have lived through a major earthquake, may wish

to move away from the edge of their home plate.

Assignment

Proofread the following paragraph for nonstandard pronoun forms. There are eight of them. Then make the necessary corrections.

Anyone who is as afraid of sickness as me should devote some of their time to reading Norman Cousins' book *Anatomy of an Illness.* Mr. Cousins, who is editor of the magazine *Saturday Review,* became seriously ill in 1964. Nearly paralyzed, he entered the hospital in excruciating pain. None of the doctors who he consulted could help him. As each of them presented their diagnosis, Cousins sank deeper into despair. Apparently he had a degenerative disease of the spine that could not be cured. None of the drugs eased his pain, although each had their own negative side effects. The doctors despaired, but Cousins refused to be as fatalistic as them. He checked himself out of the hospital and into a hotel. There he followed a carefully planned diet and took Vitamin C intravenously. Believing that stress and negativity might be causing his disease, he decided to replace it with laughter and positivity. Every day he watched films of the Marx Brothers and "Candid Camera" to make himself laugh. The more he laughed, the less pain he felt, and the better he got. Today Mr. Cousins is fully recovered. No one seems to have demonstrated more vividly than him that laughter is the best medicine.

Chapter 12

Commas

Commas signal important boundaries within sentences. By separating one word, phrase, or clause from another, or by enclosing a word, phrase, or clause, commas function to make meaning clear and to prevent misreading. Where no misreading is possible, and where no pause in speaking the sentence is natural, usually no comma is needed. These simple generalizations sum up all of the most important conventions for the use of the comma.

Pretest: Commas

Commas have been omitted in most of the sentences below. Keeping in mind that commas mark important pauses and prevent misreading, add commas where they are necessary.

1. Many bicycle riders prefer a ten-speed to a single-speed bike for climbing hills is much easier with a choice of gears.
2. An efficient ten-speed bicycle immediately offers the beginner pleasant riding and touring cross-country may soon follow.
3. In addition to the variable gears ten-speed bicycles have carefully engineered frames to cut down on weight.
4. Although it is possible to spend a great deal of money buying a good bicycle does not have to cost a lot.
5. Many ten-speed bicycles do not have fenders kick stands or chain guards.
6. Older adults have begun to ride bicycles for transportation for recreation for exercise or for all three.
7. The Windsor AM-5 International an excellent bike costs less than $250.

8. The lightest ten-speed bicycles which are also the most expensive are easiest to peddle.
9. Bicycles that cost over $700 are too expensive for Pat.
10. She would like to buy a bicycle but she can only afford a used one.

12a Commas That Separate

12a(1) Separating Main Clauses Joined by a Coordinating Conjunction

A comma should separate two or more main clauses (independent clauses) joined by a coordinating conjunction (*and, but, or, nor, for, yet, so, either . . . or, neither . . . nor, not only . . . but also*). The comma precedes the conjunction.

> Many bicycle riders prefer a ten-speed to a single-speed bike, for climbing hills is much easier with a choice of gears.

Without the comma and the pause it signals, the sentence is likely to be initially misread as

> Many bicycle riders prefer a ten-speed to a single-speed bike for climbing hills . . .

The comma is necessary to convey the intended meaning clearly.

> An efficient ten-speed bicycle immediately offers the beginner pleasant riding, and touring cross-country may soon follow.

If the comma is omitted from this sentence, a reader may miss the separation between the two main clauses joined by *and,* at first misreading the sentence as

> An efficient ten-speed bicycle immediately offers the beginner pleasant riding and touring cross-country . . .

The comma is essential to prevent misreading.

Very short clauses joined by a coordinating conjunction need no commas.

Tires hummed and chrome glistened.

Although two clauses joined by a coordinating conjunction should be separated by a comma, two words or two phrases joined by a coordinating conjunction need *not* be separated by a comma.

Many ten-speed bicycles do not have <u>fenders</u> or <u>kick stands</u>.

Adults ride <u>for recreation</u> and <u>for exercise</u>.

12a(2) Separating Introductory Phrases

A comma should separate an introductory part of a sentence from what follows, especially if the absence of a comma might result in misreading.

In addition to the variable gears, ten-speed bicycles have carefully engineered frames to cut down on weight.

If no comma followed the introductory phrase *In addition to the variable gears,* this sentence would be much more difficult to interpret. It might be initially misread as

In addition to the variable gears ten-speed bicycles have . . .

Without a comma, reading the following sentence correctly becomes difficult.

Although it is possible to spend a great deal of money, buying a good bicycle does not have to cost a lot.

Without the comma, this sentence might be misread at first as

Although it is possible to spend a great deal of money buying a good bicycle . . .

As shown in this example, a comma is usually required after a dependent clause (*Although it is possible to spend a great deal of money*) that precedes a main clause (*buying a good bicycle does not have to cost a lot*).

Where there is no possibility of misreading, the comma may be omitted after a single, brief introductory word or short phrase.

CLEAR: First, I checked the tires.

ALSO CLEAR: First I checked the tires.

CLEAR: At noon, the rally began.

ALSO CLEAR: At noon the rally began.

12a(3) Separating Items in a Series

Where three or more items occur in a list, called a *series,* commas should separate them.

> Many ten-speed bicycles do not have fenders, kick stands, or chain guards.

Commas go between the nouns that make up the series *fenders, kick stands, or chain guards.*

> The red, green, and gold frame pleased her.

Commas separate the adjectives in the list *red, green, and gold.*

When phrases occur in a series of three or more, they too are separated by commas.

> Older adults have begun to ride bicycles for transportation, for recreation, for exercise, or for all three.

> The students rode their bikes to the building, carried them up the stairs, and locked them in the storeroom.

Commas also should separate independent clauses in a series of three or more.

> Tires hummed, chrome glistened, and bells rang.

12a(4) Separating Dates, Addresses, and Titles

In dates, commas should separate the day, the date of the month, and the year.

> Sunday, January 24, 1952, was her birthday.

In addresses, commas should separate the name, the street address, the name of the city, and the name of the state.

> Send the check to Time Inc., 3435 Wilshire Boulevard, Los Angeles, California 90010, before May 30. (No comma separates the state from the zip code.)

Commas should separate titles and degrees that follow names. No comma separates a title when it precedes the name.

> John Clark, Ph.D., President, announced the resignation of Associate Dean Maloney.

12a(5) Separating Expressions from Direct Quotations

Commas should separate expressions like *he said, she answered,* and *she remarked* from direct quotations. Commas following a direct quotation always go inside the quotation marks.

> "Here are the samples," she said, "if you want them." He replied, "I don't want them."

When the direct quotation ends in its own punctuation, then no comma is used.

> "Not necessarily!" she exclaimed.

Exercise 12.1 | Insert commas where they are necessary in the sentences below.

1. Old Faithful is a spectacular tourist attraction but it could be the site of a volcanic eruption.
2. Two and a half million visitors come each year to see the geysers the bubbling mud holes and the hot-water lakes in Yellowstone National Park.
3. Although tourists to Yellowstone may find the natural phenomena around them entertaining and beautiful the underground forces that energize the geysers are awesome and potentially dangerous.
4. Molten rock at 1300 degrees Fahrenheit underlies the park but scientists disagree about where the rock comes from.
5. Cold rainwater seeps down through cracks faults and fissures in the ground.
6. As it nears the reservoir of molten rock the water is heated and the hot water and steam then hiss upwards.
7. When geophysicists compared recent geodetic surveys of the park with those done in 1923 they discovered that the central portion of the park had risen over 2 feet.
8. During his lecture at the university on Wednesday January 26 1982 J. R. Belson M.A. said "Any increase in earthquake activity

could point to a violent unpredictable and extremely dangerous future for Yellowstone."
9. Whatever the long range dangers of "the Yellowstone bulge" Old Faithful's hourly displays are continuing on schedule for the present.
10. Certainly mysterious the earth puts on a show but the audience must beware.

12b Commas That Enclose

12b(1) Enclosing Nonrestrictive Clauses

Pairs of commas should enclose clauses and phrases that are not essential to the central meaning of the sentence.

My Uncle John, who lives in Amboy, mines gold for a living.

The clause *who lives in Amboy* is called *nonrestrictive* because the information in it is not essential to the basic meaning of the sentence. In fact, the clause set off by commas can be removed from the sentence without altering the central meaning: "My Uncle John mines gold for a living."
If the commas were omitted, however, the sentence would seem to say that I have more than one Uncle John.

My Uncle John who lives in Amboy mines gold for a living.

But that is not the meaning intended by the original sentence.

The Windsor AM-5 International, an excellent bike, costs less than $250.

The phrase set off by commas, *an excellent bike,* is nonrestrictive. It is not necesssary for the basic meaning of the sentence and could be omitted with only a loss of incidental information: "The Windsor AM-5 International costs less than $250."
Phrases and clauses that *are* essential to the basic meaning of the sentence should *not* be set off from the rest of the sentence with commas.

Bicycles that cost over $700 are too expensive for Pat.

The relative pronoun *that* introduces clauses containing essential information. The relative pronoun *which* introduces clauses containing nonessential information. The clause *that cost over $700* is called *restrictive* because the information in it is an important part of the central meaning of the sentence. Without this clause, the meaning of the sentence changes significantly: "Bicycles are too expensive for Pat." The original sentence stated that only bicycles costing more than $700 were out of Pat's reach. To express that meaning, the clause must not have commas around it.

If the sentence were written with commas enclosing the clause, not only would the sentence have a different meaning, but it would also no longer be true. It would seem to say that all bicycles cost over $700.

Bicycles, which cost over $700, are too expensive for Pat.

Now the sentence claims all bikes are too expensive for Pat, just as it did when we omitted the modifying clause entirely.

Commas enclose phrases and clauses that add only incidental information and are not essential to the basic meaning. If the clause or phrase *is* essential, no commas set it off.

NOT ESSENTIAL: The U.S. Constitution, which guarantees individual freedoms, ought to be more carefully studied.

Since there is only one U.S. Constitution, the clause *which guarantees individual freedoms* is not necessary to clarify which constitution ought to be more carefully studied. Commas are necessary.

ESSENTIAL: The constitution that our club just adopted forbids chewing tobacco.

The clause *that our club just adopted* is needed to identify which constitution is being talked about. No commas enclose essential clauses.

NOT ESSENTIAL: My first bicycle, a rusty clunker, sits unused in the garage.

The phrase *a rusty clunker* is descriptive, but it is not required to identify which bicycle is under discussion. Therefore it is set off in commas.

ESSENTIAL: My cousin Betty graduated from law school.

Betty is essential to the meaning of the sentence and is therefore not enclosed in commas.

NOT ESSENTIAL: Betty Smith, my youngest cousin, graduated from law school.

The phrase *my youngest cousin* adds incidental information, but it is not essential to the central meaning of the sentence, so it is set off from the rest of the sentence with commas.

Sometimes a phrase or clause might be either essential or nonessential. Then commas, or the absence of them, are the reader's only means of knowing what the sentence means.

Crossword puzzles that are difficult fascinate Sharon.

This means "Difficult crossword puzzles fascinate Sharon." The clause *that are difficult* is essential (restrictive).

Crossword puzzles, which are difficult, fascinate Sharon.

This means "All crossword puzzles fascinate Sharon; crossword puzzles are difficult." The clause *which are difficult* is nonessential (nonrestrictive).

12b(2)   Enclosing Parenthetical Expressions

Whenever a nonessential word or phrase interrupts the flow of the sentence, it may be enclosed in commas to indicate a pause.

Betty has not, <u>however</u>, found a job yet.

She has not, <u>in fact</u>, begun to look for one.

She said, <u>without meaning to hurt his feelings</u>, that he looked ghastly.

Such a word or phrase that is not part of the main sentence, but that contains information or makes a comment that the writer wishes to insert into the sentence, is called a *parenthetical expression*.

12b(3)   Enclosing Names in Direct Address

When a sentence is addressed directly to a person who is named, the name should be enclosed in commas.

I must agree, Bill, that you're very clever.

If you wish, Professor, we can type our term papers.

Exercise 12.2 | Add commas where they are required in the sentences below.

1. The bottom of the ocean an environment in which it is extremely difficult for humans to work offers an abundance of minerals.
2. Vast areas of the seabed are littered with blackish lumps called *manganese nodules.*
3. These manganese nodules which often lie at depths of up to 20,000 feet contain more than forty elements.
4. Manganese an extremely valuable mineral constitutes up to 30 percent of some of the nodules.
5. Nickel copper and cobalt which are also valuable are present in concentrations many times higher than in land ores.
6. Deepsea Ventures a company dedicated to mining the ocean floors hopes to retrieve millions of tons of mineral lumps.
7. One problem that faces companies like Deepsea Ventures is to determine who owns minerals located under international waters.
8. The United Nations which is attempting to create international controls over the exploitation of the ocean floors has drafted a Law of the Sea treaty.
9. This treaty hotly debated since its inception declares that the nodules are the heritage of all people.
10. The U.N. Law of the Sea a very controversial proposal would guarantee royalties to less developed countries. However the companies that have invested in deep-sea mining technology feel entitled to profit from their investment.

Recap

1. Commas should separate sentences joined by a coordinating conjunction.

   Bicycles provide good exercise, and they get the best gas mileage possible.

2. Commas should separate an introductory part of a sentence from what follows.

   In addition to the variable gears, ten-speed bicycles have carefully engineered frames.

3. Commas should separate three or more items in a series.

Adults ride bicycles for transportation, for recreation, for exercise, or for all three.

Two items are not separated by a comma.

Adults ride for recreation and for exercise.

4. Commas should separate the divisions of dates, addresses, and names with titles.

Sunday, January 24, 1952, faded from memory.

The letter was addressed to National Bank, 761 Main Street, Midtown, Connecticut 06042.

John Clark, Ph.D., President, welcomed the delegates.

5. Commas enclose nonrestrictive modifiers and other nonessential parts of sentences.

Uncle John, who lives in Amboy, mines gold.

The Windsor AM-5 International, an excellent bike, costs less than $250.

Betty has not, however, found a job yet.

Essential parts of sentences are not set off by commas.

Bicycles that cost over $750 are too expensive for Pat.

6. Commas enclose names used in direct address.

I have asked you several times, Charles, to return my typewriter.

7. Commas separate direct quotations from expressions like *she said.*

"My pencil broke," she said.

8. Commas enclose parenthetical expressions.

Jim argued, in other words, for a promotion.

Posttest: Commas

Insert commas where they are required in the sentences below.

1. Serious illness and death are subjects many people would like to avoid but everyone must face them sooner or later.

2. Carl and Stephanie Simonton who train counselors of the sick and dying do not approach the human problems of illness and death with pessimism or despair.

3. Because they believe that emotional factors have a lot to do with who gets sick and who recovers the Simontons have developed techniques for helping people to deal with the emotional side of illness.

4. Getting a disease like cancer they believe is one way certain people respond to stress. By learning to understand themselves and their responses to stress cancer patients can learn to participate actively in their own treatment.

5. Carl Simonton a physician trained in radiation treatment of cancer came to believe that despair reduced a cancer patient's chance of recovery. After hearing a diagnosis of cancer some patients just resign themselves to treatment but others seem to have active hope and optimism.

6. The Simontons believe that counseling can help terminally ill patients to live longer to have fewer side effects from their treatments and to die more peacefully than if they passively surrender to medical treatment alone.

7. At a retreat center in Briarwood Texas counselors learn how to use relaxation techniques play-therapy and methods of visualizing one's body fighting cancer cells.

8. The Simontons' methods of treatment which are to be employed along with traditional medical treatments aim at reducing repression denial and depression.

9. According to the Simontons cancer patients who do well under medical treatment have a strong self-concept and are emotionally resilient physically active flexible in their beliefs and socially autonomous.

10. The Simontons' beliefs are not accepted by most of the medical community yet they are finding an increasing acceptance among patients and counselors.

Assignment

Proofread the following paragraph. Circle unnecessary commas that should be removed. Insert commas where they are required.

In colonial America heat meant a fireplace, or a wood stove. By 1970 however heating systems, that run on electricity oil or natural gas had become just about universal. Wood heated only a small percentage of American homes mostly those of rural families with their own wood supplies. But then came the oil embargo, and the end of the era of cheap energy. The price of home-heating oil soared, and the demand for wood stoves soared right along with it. Even though wood stoves have undergone a resurgence in popularity they are not likely to replace conventional home-heating equipment, for most people. They are not practical in apartments, for example, or in houses, with many rooms to heat. Unless there is a convenient source nearby wood is not cheap. Anyone, who wants to heat with a wood stove, will have to have a woodpile in the back yard and will have to split logs, and carry them indoors. Stoves take up a lot of space and they must be tended constantly. Chimneys must be swept and ashes have to be cleaned up, and taken out. To Americans, who are the satisfied owners of wood stoves, these problems are apparently unimportant. The wood-burning stove which once seemed to be an endangered species is once again a functional part of many American homes.

Chapter 13

Semicolons and Colons

The most important use of semicolons is to separate closely related main clauses that are not joined by a coordinating conjunction such as *and, or,* or *but.*

> The telephone rang; Linda answered it.

The most important use of colons is to introduce a list (a series), an explanation, or a direct quotation following an otherwise complete sentence.

> Bob's knowledge of cooking is limited to three dishes: boiled eggs, fried eggs, and scrambled eggs. (series)
>
> The reason for his absence was simple: his car wouldn't start. (explanation)
>
> Geraldine spoke sharply to her dog: "Sit!" (quotation)

After you check your understanding of the conventions for the use of semicolons and colons in the Pretest, we will review, and give you practice with, their major uses.

Pretest: Semicolons and Colons

Insert semicolons and colons where they are appropriate in the sentences below.

1. The duckbill platypus is an unusual animal indeed, the more we study it, the odder it gets.
2. For a furry mammal, the platypus reproduces in a strange way it lays eggs.

3. The platypus's bill is rubbery skin stretched over bone its ears are in furrows just behind its eyes.
4. The platypus lives and feeds in rivers and lakes however, it sleeps in burrows in the bank.
5. When submerged, the platypus uses its sensitive bill to locate insect larvae, crayfish, and small frogs on land it dines on worms.
6. The first European naturalists to report on the platypus described the Australian creature in strange ways an amphibious mole, a miniature otter, a beaver with a beak, and a combination of a fish, bird, and quadruped.
7. One difficulty faced by early naturalists still troubles biologists today the platypus is both a creature of dusky hours and extremely wary of humans.
8. Besides their descriptions of this strange creature, the early visitors to Australia sent back reports of some other extraordinary wildlife enormous hopping animals with pouches, tiny arms, and large tails huge burrowing guinea pigs, called *wombats,* which were said to be fierce in battle as well as tasty in stew spiny anteaters which, like the platypus, were egg-laying mammals.
9. Today, more than two hundred years after the platypus was first observed scientifically, researchers who study the creature must still respond to many questions about the platypus with a cautious answer "We really don't know."
10. Next time you visit the zoo, don't miss the oddest creature of all the duckbill platypus.

13a Semicolons

13a(1) Separating Closely Related Main Clauses

When two main clauses are closely related in meaning but are not linked by a coordinating conjunction such as *and, but, or, nor, for, so,* and *yet,* they may be separated by a semicolon.

> When submerged, the platypus eats insect larvae, crayfish, and small frogs; on land it dines on worms.

A period could replace the semicolon, thereby dividing the two clauses into separate sentences.

When submerged, the platypus eats insect larvae, crayfish, and small frogs. On land it dines on worms.

Since the semicolon is not as strong a separator as the period, the two clauses seem more closely linked when only a semicolon separates them.

Semicolons are used conventionally only to separate constructions that are equal: two sentences, for example, or three phrases in a complex list. They should not appear between unequal constructions, such as between a sentence and a phrase.

INCORRECT: The platypus swims well; with webbed feet.

The phrase *with webbed feet* should not be separated from the rest of the sentence by any punctuation.

INCORRECT: On their hind legs the males have spurs; that are equipped with venom glands.

No punctuation should separate the restrictive clause *that are equipped with venom glands* from the rest of the sentence.

The relationship between the clauses separated by the semicolon may be signaled by a transitional word or phrase such as *consequently, however, indeed, moreover, nevertheless, then, therefore, thus, in fact, on the contrary,* or *on the other hand.* The transitional word follows the semicolon.

The platypus is an unusual animal; indeed, the more we study it, the odder it gets.

The transitional word or phrase may also go elsewhere in the second clause.

The platypus lives and feeds in rivers and lakes; it sleeps, however, in burrows on the banks.

13a(2) Separating Items in Complex Lists

Semicolons may be used for the sake of clarity in complex lists (series) of three or more where the phrases or clauses being listed have commas or other punctuation inside them.

The early visitors to Australia sent back reports of extraordinary wildlife: enormous hopping animals with pouches, tiny arms, and large tails; huge burrowing guinea pigs, called wombats, which were said to be fierce in battle as well as tasty in stew; spiny anteaters, which, like the platypus, were egg-laying mammals.

Exercise 13.1 | Insert semicolons where they are appropriate in the sentences below.

1. California's Mono Lake is not only dying it is, in fact, being killed by the relentless thirst for water in Los Angeles, 300 miles to the south.
2. The lake has existed for 700,000 years its future, however, may be relatively short.
3. Mono Lake has no outlet as a result, its water is more than twice as salty as the ocean's.
4. In spite of its high mineral content, the lake is rich in certain kinds of life: brine shrimp, which thrive in its salty water brine flies, which dot its shore line and algae, which grow on its sur-face and in its depths. The shrimp and flies feed on the algae birds, in turn, consume the shrimp and flies.
5. As the lake shrinks, it becomes more salty. At some point, scien-tists believe, it will be too salty for the shrimp, flies, or algae to survive in it then the hundreds of thousands of birds will disappear as well.

13b Colons

13b(1) Introducing Examples, Quotations, Explanations, and Lists

After a main clause, a colon may introduce an example or illustration in the form of a word, phrase, or clause or a list of any of these.

> Among the platypus's unusual traits, one feature is perhaps most striking of all: its duck-like bill.

In the same way, a colon may introduce a quotation after an otherwise com-plete sentence.

> Many questions about the platypus still receive the same answer from scientists: "We really don't know."

A colon may introduce a list after an otherwise complete sentence.

> Australia is the home of a number of extraordinary creatures: kangaroos, wombats, wallabies, kookaburras, echidnas, and platypuses.

A colon should not be used directly after a verb, where it would separate the verb from its object.

INCORRECT: We saw: a kangaroo, a platypus, and a wombat.

CORRECT: We saw a kangaroo, a platypus, and a wombat.

CORRECT: We saw three animals: a kangaroo, a platypus, and a wombat.

INCORRECT: The animal's favorite foods are: insect larvae, crayfish, frogs, and worms.

CORRECT: The animal's favorite foods are insect larvae, crayfish, frogs, and worms.

CORRECT: The animal has four favorite foods: insect larvae, crayfish, frogs, and worms.

Nor should colons follow directly after prepositions, where they would separate the prepositions from their objects.

INCORRECT: Early visitors sent back reports about: kangaroos, wombats, echidnas, and platypuses.

CORRECT: Early visitors sent back reports about kangaroos, wombats, echidnas, and platypuses.

CORRECT: Early visitors sent back reports about strange creatures: kangaroos, wombats, echidnas, and platypuses.

In other words, colons are used in this introductory way only after an otherwise complete sentence.

13b(2)   In Time Designations and Greetings in Formal Letters

A colon should separate the hour and minutes in time designations.

Harold's bus arrived at 3:45 A.M.

In formal business letters, a colon should follow the greeting.

Dear Sir:

Dear Senator Cranston:

Exercise 13.2 | Insert colons where they are appropriate in the sentences below.

1. By combining a hang glider with a small motor, John Moody created a new kind of aircraft the *ultralight*.

2. Taking off in an ultralight is strenuous the pilot must run headlong down the runway with the plane on his back.

3. Ultralight aircraft meld a variety of diverse components stainless steel aircraft cable, Dacron sailcloth, plastic hang glider fittings, pop rivets, bicycle wheels, and lawn mower throttles.

4. Not everyone can afford one of these minimal airplanes they cost between three and four thousand dollars.

5. Although ultralight planes may not be a practical solution to an earthbound commuter's frustrations, they do offer exactly what their original inventors sought the sensuous freedom of flight. Given the chance to launch myself into the sky with one of these lightweight machines, I would have only one response "Hand me a parachute!"

Recap

1. Semicolons may separate closely related main clauses.

   Mono Lake has no outlet; as a result, its water is extremely salty.

2. Semicolons may separate items in complex lists.

   The lake is rich in certain kinds of life: brine shrimp, which thrive in its salty water; brine flies, which dot its shore line; and algae, which grow on its surface and in its depths.

3. Semicolons should not separate sentences from phrases or clauses.

   INCORRECT: The platypus swims well; with webbed feet.

   INCORRECT: On their hind legs, the males have spurs; that are equipped with venom glands.

4. Colons should follow a complete sentence to signal the introduction of an example, an explanation, a quotation, or a list.

   The platypus resembles a reptile in one way: it lays eggs.

   Naturalists are forced to give the same old answer: "We don't really know."

   Australia is home to some unusual creatures: kangaroos, wombats. wallabies, and echidnas.

5. Colons should not follow a verb or a preposition.

INCORRECT: We saw: a kangaroo, a platypus, and a wombat.

INCORRECT: Early visitors sent reports about: kangaroos, wombats, and echidnas.

6. Colons should appear in time designations and after greetings in formal letters.

We open at 9:00 A.M.

Dear Madam:

Posttest: Semicolons and Colons

Insert semicolons and colons where they are appropriate in the sentences below.

1. Lending money to developing countries is the sole job of one important institution the World Bank.
2. The World Bank does not provide checking or savings accounts for individuals rather, it directs multimillion-dollar loans for world development.
3. The magnitude of World Bank lending is huge it has loaned $85 billion in its thirty-five-year history.
4. In its early years, the World Bank concentrated on large-scale projects building hydroelectric plants, roads, and railways boosting production, both agricultural and industrial, for export and modernizing industry.
5. Today the Bank pays equal attention to projects that directly help the world's poor constructing irrigation systems for poor farmers in arid regions bringing pure drinking water to peasants who have all their lives had to accept intestinal diseases as a fact of life educating illiterate couples about birth control building schools and training teachers rehabilitating city slums.
6. Developing countries are sometimes referred to collectively as the "Third World" this term distinguishes them from the Western-style democracies, or "First World," and from the Soviet bloc, or "Second World."

7. World Bank funds come from two sources contributions from member governments and loans from governments and corporations.

8. Wealthy nations support the World Bank for other than simply charitable reasons indeed, the bank itself argues that economic assistance makes economic sense.

9. Improving conditions of life for the world's poorest people may make sound business sense however, supporters of the World Bank believe strongly that rich countries have a moral responsibility to assist the poor.

10. Improving living conditions in the world's poorest regions also serves another goal world peace.

Assignment

Proofread the following paragraphs. Circle any colons and semicolons that are incorrectly used. Insert colons and semicolons where they are appropriate.

One ability has long been held to be unique to humans language. But since 1969 unprecedented events have challenged this belief. The challenge has come from the linguistic accomplishments of several nonhuman primates Washoe, Sarah, Koko, Lana, and others. Washoe, a chimp, learned to use signs from American Sign Language; the gestural language of North American deaf people. Koko, a gorilla, also learned signs. Sarah, a chimpanzee, learned an artificial language "written" in colored plastic shapes; Lana learned Yerkish; a computer language. Each of these animals seemed to be able to: answer questions, follow instructions, and make requests and observations. Washoe apparently did something even more amazing she taught signs to her foster son Loulis. In addition, some of the apes were apparently able to create new and appropriate combinations of signs, which they had not been taught to do.

Critics argue that the apes have only been taught complex tricks they claim that trainers are cuing the apes rather than conversing with them. Those who feel that the apes have not really demonstrated language ability accuse their trainers of anthropomorphism: ascribing human traits to nonhumans. One group argues that the animals' behavior cannot be called language; because it doesn't show the grammatical complexity of human language. The other group insists that: something very language-like is going on in the apes' interaction with humans. Whichever view future research supports, the minds of our fellow primates have turned out to be more interesting and challenging than previously imagined.

Chapter 14

Apostrophes, Quotation Marks, and Italics

Apostrophes, quotation marks, and italics (indicated in typed and hand-written work by underlining) occur very frequently in all kinds of writing, yet even relatively experienced writers often misunderstand some of their uses. After you have checked your knowledge about them by completing the pretest, we will review a handful of simple rules that can guide you in the correct use of these important signals of meaning.

Pretest: Apostrophes, Quotation Marks, and Italics

Add apostrophes, quotation marks, and italics as necessary to make the following sentences correct. (Indicate italics by underlining.)

1. Hes too young to do the job theyve given him.
2. Vic returned the typewriter because the cs and ds stuck.
3. Most of the junior college students earned their A.A.s.
4. Mary added three P.S.s to her letter.
5. Two plants roots were cut off by the bulldozer.
6. He did an honest days work.
7. Childrens activities are not only womens responsibilities.
8. Two nurses tried to care for the babies needs.
9. The professor read Yeatss last poem.
10. They didn't seek anyones opinion.
11. Its unfortunate that the ring had lost its stone.
12. What happened? asked the stunt man, still in a daze.
13. An actor read the short story, A Rose for Emily.
14. Paul Simon wrote the song, Still Crazy after All These Years.
15. I liked his writing, except for the repetition of because.

16. Star Wars broke all box office records.
17. Samuel Johnsons Dictionary is peppered with wit.
18. She blew a kiss and an au revoir.
19. Do I have to shout that no means no?
20. Audiences still feel the emotional depth of Arthur Millers Death of a Salesman.

14a   Apostrophes

14a(1)   For Contractions

In a contraction, one or more letters are omitted; an apostrophe marks the spot at which the letter or letters have been left out.

you are = you're	they are = they're
he will = he'll	there is = there's
they have = they've	should not = shouldn't (*not* should'nt)
we would = we'd	did not = didn't (*not* did'nt)

The use of contractions makes writing seem very informal. For this reason they are used seldom, if at all, in formal writing.

Exercise 14.1 | Create contracted forms for each of the following.

1. let us   _____
2. who is   _____
3. it is   _____
4. she will   _____
5. they had   _____
6. I have   _____
7. you will   _____
8. he is   _____
9. would not   _____
10. John is here.   _____

14a(2)   For Certain Plurals

Form the plurals of abbreviations containing periods by adding *'s.*

> The company prefers to hire employees with M.A.'s.

> John celebrated the return of the P.O.W.'s.

No apostrophe should be used to form plurals of letters, numbers, or abbreviations that do not contain periods.

> *C*s are better than *D*s.

> The computer printed out ten 4s.

> Carlie has driven two VWs into the ground.

Exercise 14.2 | Write sentences in which you correctly use the plural form for each of the following.

1. VTR _____

2. X _____

3. Ph.D. _____

4. 4x4 _____

5. YWCA _____

6. 1960 _____

7. M.D. _____

8. 5 _____

9. S _____

10. B.A. _____

14a(3)   For Possessive Forms

Possessive means *belongs to.*

> The plant's roots belong to the plant.

> The shoe's laces belong to the shoe.

> The day's work belongs to the day.

A singular noun forms its possessive by adding an apostrophe and then an *s*.

> The jet's wings
>
> The guitar's strings
>
> The sun's heat

A plural noun forms its possessive by adding an apostrophe after the plural *s*. Form the plural first and then add the apostrophe indicating possession.

> Many jets' wings
>
> Many guitars' strings

Singular nouns already ending in *s* form the possessive by adding *'s*.

> The bus's windows steamed up.
>
> A chemist still must investigate the gas's properties.

A plural noun *not* ending in *s* forms the possessive by adding an apostrophe first, and then an *s*.

> Women's opportunities grew during the 1970s.
>
> He redecorated the children's room.

Possessive pronouns such as *their, theirs, your, yours, our, ours, her, hers, it,* and *its* do *not* take apostrophes. Beginning writers (and even some experienced ones) sometimes confuse *its* and *it's. Its* (without an apostrophe) means "belongs to it."

> The puppy hurt its paw.

It's (with an apostrophe) is the contraction for *it is.*

> It's the same puppy that hurt its paw.

If you are ever unsure about which form to use, try the following substitution test. Read in *it is* (or *it has*) when you don't know whether to use *its* or *it's*. If *it is* (or *it has*) sounds right, use an apostrophe. If *it is* (or *it has*) sounds wrong, don't use an apostrophe.

Let's say that you have written "It's been a long time since summer." You are not sure of the *It's.* Substitute *It has* in place of *It's.* Now the sentence reads, "It has been a long time since summer." Since the sentence sounds fine and the substitution has not changed its meaning, the apostrophe is correct. In the case of "The puppy hurt its paw," the substitution would not have worked. Neither *it is paw* nor *it has paw* makes sense in the sentence; hence, no apostrophe should be used.

Such pronouns as *anyone* and *everyone* form possessives by adding *'s.*

They didn't seek anyone's opinion.

They eloped, to everyone's surprise.

Exercise 14.3 | Write in the correct possessive form of the word shown, changing singular to plural if necessary.

1. (hummingbird) Johnson photographed the _____ nest.

2. (Gershwin) The conductor had a special affection for _____ music.

3. (refrigerator) The quality control inspector refused to pass those three _____ door seals.

4. (baby) Two nurses tried to care for ten _____ needs.

5. (newspaper) He managed to persuade the _____ editor.

6. (elevator) Quickly she scanned two _____ occupants, seeking her friend's face.

7. (doughnut) Frankly, we preferred not to know the _____ ingredients.

8. (train) The mine superintendent mapped out the three _____ destinations.

9. (business) The report glamorized the _____ profits.

10. (asparagus) She disliked the _____ texture.

11. (mice) Morley sealed off the _____ holes.

12. (lass) He wore the _____ ribbon through a buttonhole.

13. (Keats) Our reading group is studying _____ poetry.

14. (someone) Jerry found _____ class ring.

15. (her) The ring was definitely _____ .

16. (it) Unfortunately, the ring had lost _____ stone.

17. (your) Perhaps the ring is _____ .

18. (no one) The loss was _____ fault.

19. (waitress) The restaurant owner took half of both _____

    tips.

20. (Los Angeles) Farley would like to be _____ mayor.

14b   Quotation Marks

14b(1)   For Direct Quotations

Quotation marks are used, first, to separate someone else's exact words from your own.

> She cried, "I've found the solution!"

> "What happened?" asked the stunt man, still dazed.

(In research papers, long quotations may be identified as someone else's words by indenting them from the rest of the text, rather than by placing them in quotation marks.)

Remember these three hints for using other punctuation marks with direct quotations:

> Periods and commas always go inside the quotation marks at the ends of quotations.

> "Don't bother," the waiter said.

> Exclamation marks and question marks go inside the quotation marks only when they are part of the quotation.

> INSIDE: Harry wondered out loud, "Why me?"

> OUTSIDE: Did Jill really say, "I'll think about it"?

Colons and semicolons go outside quotation marks.

Bill said, "She'll sing soprano"; however, Jill replied, "I'll think about it."

When one direct quotation contains another, the second quotation is set off by single quotation marks.

Miranda corrected me by saying, "Jim said 'Niel's son,' not 'Nielson.' "

Notice that the final period is inside both the single and the double quotation marks.

Exercise 14.4 | Combine each of the following pairs into one sentence using quotation marks.

You Write	*Someone Else Says*
1. The captain shouted	Reef the mainsail!
2. Malcolm hesitantly asked	Are those books for sale?
3. The marshal whispered	Try me.
4. The soccer player moaned	Yes, it's a bit painful.
5. Her parents reminded her	You're only nineteen.

14b(2) For Titles of Short Works and Parts of a Book

Use quotation marks to indicate the title of a short poem, short story, song, television show, or essay or of a chapter or other part of a book.

Wordsworth wrote "We are Seven." (poem)

The actor read "A Rose for Emily." (short story)

Exercise 14.5 | Write a sentence for each of the items below. Use quotation marks correctly in referring to a title of your choice.

    1. (song) _____

    2. (poem) _____

    3. (essay) _____

    4. (short story) _____

    5. (chapter title) _____

14b(3) For Words Used in an Ironic Sense

Quotation marks may be used to enclose words used in an ironic sense. Such quotation marks mean approximately the same thing as the words *so-called,* but when *so-called,* or its equivalent, is used, the word or phrase following it should not be enclosed in quotation marks.

> That "investment counselor" is really just a salesperson.

> That so-called investment counselor is really just a salesperson.

> Salespeople are sometimes referred to as investment counselors.

Use quotation marks in this way very sparingly in formal writing.

Exercise 14.6 | Add quotation marks, if necessary, to make the following sentences correct.

1. The grizzled old sailor was affectionately known as Cap'n along the docks.
2. Merton assured the townspeople that their monster was nothing more than a crazed goat.
3. In a fuming rage, the senator rose to insist that she was not a swindler.
4. My so-called music teacher can't even read notes.
5. That money-back-guarantee resulted in several hundred people losing their investment.

14c Italics

Most typewriters do not have a special set of characters for italic print. Consequently, writers underline words that would appear in italics if the writing were professionally typeset.

14c(1) For Titles of Major Works

Use italics for titles of books, plays, movies, and newspapers.

Samuel Johnson's *Dictionary* is peppered with wit.

The theme song from *Star Wars* has been borrowed by many advertisers.

14c(2) For Foreign Words and Phrases

Use italics for foreign words that have not become part of the English language through common usage.

Maria's grandfather continued to call his pizza parlor a *ristorante.*

Pizza and *ristorante* both come from Italian, but *pizza* has become a common English word. Consult a dictionary if necessary.

14c(3) For Emphasis

You may use italics to mark emphasis or give a special tone, but do this very sparingly.

I'm certainly *not* the right person for that job.

Jacobs was interested not in what the junior college had *been,* but in what it might *become.*

14c(4) For Words or Letters Used as Such

You may use italics to refer to words as words or letters as letters.

He felt that the word *aforementioned* was too formal for the advertising circular.

She pointed out that the phrase *due to the fact that* could be replaced by *because.*

Exercise 14.7 | Indicate italics by underlining the appropriate words in the following sentences.

1. In Harold's opinion, the raison d'etre of a college education is meeting girls.
2. Fear and Loathing in Las Vegas made me laugh, cringe, and shudder all at the same time.
3. Each of his firm promises was followed by but.
4. The clever banter on M.A.S.H. owes much to Groucho Marx.
5. The letter j is a late addition to the alphabet.
6. The salesperson needed to be told emphatically that no means no.
7. With teary eyes the family gathered in the cold mist to say a last auf Wiedersehen.
8. Expecting a mere sea story, he picked Moby Dick off the shelf.
9. Bleary-eyed, the kids at the slumber party tried to stay up for Saturday Night Live.
10. The motto of the Prince of Wales—ich dien—means "I serve."

Recap

1. Apostrophes mark missing letters in contractions.

   isn't   they've   I'll

2. Apostrophes are used to form some plurals.

   C.O.D.'s   M.A.'s   P.S.'s

3. Apostrophes indicate possession.

   SINGULAR: plant's   someone's   bus's
   PLURAL: plants'   children's

   Remember
   it's = it is
   its = possessive

4. Quotation marks should separate others' words from your own.

   He shouted, "Here I am!"

5. Quotation marks should set off titles of short poems, short stories, songs, chapters, or essays.

   "Kubla Khan"   "Where Have All the Flowers Gone"

6. Quotation marks may be used to indicate irony.

   The "facts" you heard are really just gossip.

7. Use italics (or underlining) to mark the titles of books, plays, movies, and newspapers.

   Star Wars   *Los Angeles Times*

8. Use italics to identify foreign words and phrases.

   We visited a *ristorante.*

9. Italics may be used to give special emphasis.

   I've told you she's *not* the one.

10. Use italics to set off words used as words.

    Omit the *and* in the third sentence.

Posttest: Apostrophes, Quotation Marks, and Italics

Add any necessary apostrophes, quotation marks, and italics to the following sentences. Not all sentences require additions.

1. After your years of labor, you had the right to expect something.
2. The womens conversation grew animated.
3. Its about time you arrived.
4. The two boys poles broke in just the same spot.
5. This memory is hers alone.
6. General Transistor Corporation was only hiring M.A.s.
7. He tucked a dog-eared copy of The Sun Also Rises under his arm.
8. The leader asked, Where is O'Toole?
9. Hes about the same height as she is.
10. The puppy shook loose its collar.
11. The word seems casts doubt over your whole essay.
12. Did the leader say, There is O'Toole?
13. Blake wrote the short poem, The Tyger.
14. I think that someones purse was left behind.
15. Fill in your questionnaire with Xs.
16. We had to remember to substitute gracias for merci.
17. Probably the best way to describe the blind date is to say that it was different.

18. The boys pole snapped just above the reel.
19. Please sing Scarborough Fair.
20. Youve considered both sides of the issue.

Assignment

Edit the following paragraph so that apostrophes, quotation marks, and italics are correctly used.

In his book "Adventure on a Shoestring," Peter Alicante gives advice to student's who want to travel abroad without much money. His first chapter, Theres a Trip to Fit Everyones Wallet, includes the usual advice about charter flights and youth hostels. The books four longest chapters focus on Europe, Africa, Asia, and South America. However, his best chapter is the last one, "How to Get the Most Out of Foreign Travel". Here Mr. Alicante says, Any foreign travel is more enjoyable and worthwhile if one is prepared to travel with a pleasant tolerance of differences in customs, living standards, habits, and schedules. He then tells the stories of several different students' mishaps and disappointments, each of which he attributes to the ignorance and intolerance of the travelers toward the countries in which they were guests. "Its a shame", he concludes, "that these students' failed to learn the lessons that travel teaches. Alicante's concluding sentences express the central theme of his book: "Ive visited 103 countries on every continent. Wherever I've gone, the key to my enjoyment and learning has been my appreciation for the differences between my culture and that of other's."

Chapter 15

Parentheses, Dashes, and Hyphens

Parentheses [( )], dashes (—), and hyphens (-) appear more and more commonly in modern writing. Both rules and the writer's judgment govern their use. After you evaluate your own judgment with respect to these marks by completing the Pretest, we will give you practice in making appropriate decisions about when to use them.

Pretest: Parentheses, Dashes, and Hyphens

Place parentheses, dashes, and hyphens where they belong in the following sentences.

1. The bat a symbolic animal for several Native American peoples is depicted in Inca mosaics, jewelry, and statuary.
2. Photosynthesis the action of sunlight upon chlorophyll may soon be synthetically duplicated in the laboratory.
3. Fifty eight fish lay rotting in the hold of the old trawler now in dry dock.
4. The early Romantic poets Blake, Wordsworth, Coleridge shared an interest in the workings of human emotion.
5. At thirty two he was a bit too old to inhabit a mental never never land.
6. The Mexican sombrero a wide-brimmed hat was often decorated with ancestral emblems.
7. The group finally elected Harrison who, by the way, voted for his opponent.
8. Marta Jenson's candidacy the only hope for change in the legislature is to be announced publicly tomorrow.
9. Smooth, rounded rocks the kind found in stream beds provide attractive ground cover for garden areas and entries.
10. My father in law stood ankle deep in the mud.

15a   Parentheses

15a(1)   For Definitions or Explanatory Details

Parentheses can enclose explanations, explanatory details, or definitions.

> The bat (a symbolic animal for several Native American tribes) is depicted in Inca mosaics, jewelry, and statuary.

> The first chapter of our linguistics textbook deals with phonemes (the sounds in a language that distinguish one word from another), but most of the class failed to read it.

Parentheses are *misused* when they enclose comments that should have been included in the main statement. See section 5m for a discussion of this error.

Exercise 15.1   Use parentheses to provide a brief definition in the space provided. Use your dictionary as necessary.

1. Deciduous trees _____

    lined the long walk from the cabin to the lake.

2. The sensation of *ennui* _____

    is valued by some philosophers as a sane response to life's

    difficulties.

3. Igneous rock _____ led

    the geologists to the fault itself.

4. Leukemia _____ may

    become a curable disease within this generation.

5. *Deuteronomy* _____ lists

    elaborate rules for the Israelites.

15a(2)   For Publication Information

In footnotes, parentheses are used to enclose publication information.

Malcolm Donald, *The Energy Crisis* (New York: Benson Press, 1976), p. 274.

15b Dashes

15b(1) To Separate a Series

A dash can separate a series from the rest of the sentence.

The early Romantic poets—Blake, Wordsworth, Coleridge—shared an interest in the workings of human emotion.

The dash is about twice as long as a hyphen and is typed as two hyphens (--).

Exercise 15.2 | Insert a brief list by means of dashes in the space provided.

1. Famous sports figures _____ rarely publicize their salaries and bonuses.

2. Exotic foods _____ sometimes bring exotic gastrointestinal sensations.

3. Luxurious gifts _____ tumbled from the arms of the old suitor.

4. Fast sports cars _____ require steady, expert maintenance.

5. Some Central American countries _____ _____ face the simultaneous threats of economic disaster and political overthrow.

15b(2) To Signal an Afterthought

A dash can signal an afterthought, something a writer wishes to include as if it were an idea that occurred later than the main idea of the sentence and is being added on. This use of the dash has the effect of intentionally delaying part of what the writer has to say.

Contemporary science fiction has millions of readers—including professors of literature.

The group finally elected Harrison—who, by the way, voted for his opponent.

Exercise 15.3 | Add an appropriate afterthought, marking it off by a dash.

1. Love can be unsettling _____

   _____

2. Cambridge at first seemed depressing _____

   _____

3. Newspapers provide a sampling of world news _____

   _____

4. The novice skier surveyed the long, steep hill _____

   _____

5. The farmer thought it prudent to plant two kinds of peaches _____

   _____

15b(3)   To Separate a Parenthetical Comment

Dashes can also separate parenthetical material from the rest of a sentence. In this use, the dashes set off and emphasize a comment or explanation that the writer wishes to insert.

Smooth, rounded rocks—the kind found in stream beds—provide attractive ground cover for garden areas and entries.

Exercise 15.4 | Insert an appropriate comment, setting off your addition by dashes.

1. The remnants of the flood _____

   _____ lay along the eroded highway.

2. Travelers of many nationalities _____

   _____ rushed past one another in Grand Central Station.

3. The louder instruments of the pep band _____

_____ were placed together on one side of the

stage.

4. Renaldo saved the more exciting colors _____

_____ for his new collection of evening wear.

5. Professional people _____

crowded the seminar to learn of new tax loopholes.

15c   Hyphens

15c(1)   For Compound Words and Numbers

The hyphen marks divisions within some compound words. It is not always easy to decide whether to hyphenate a compound, write it as a solid word, or write it as two words, and it is best to consult your dictionary.

Hyphenated	*One Word*	*Two Words*
water-repellent	waterproof	water rat
cat's-eye	cattail	cat's cradle
sun-god	sundown	sun deck

Compound numbers from twenty-one to ninety-nine take hyphens, as do fractions when they are spelled out.

Hyphenated	*Not Hyphenated*
forty-two bananas	one hundred chickens
seventy-six years	two thousand dollars
two-thirds of an ounce	a third of the cheese

BUT: one hundred forty-two miles
two and one-half miles

15c(2)   For Line-End Word Division

Often a word must be divided at the end of one line and continued on the next line. Divide words between syllables. A dictionary will guide you—don't guess. Examples of such division points are *bi·o·de·grad·a·ble* and *fu·tu·ri·ty*.

Exercise 15.5

1. Search the dictionary for five hyphenated compound words not listed above. Write them in the space provided.

   _____   _____

   _____   _____

   _____

2. Write out five numbers between twenty-one and ninety-nine. Place hyphens correctly.

   _____   _____

   _____   _____

   _____

3. Decide, with the help of your dictionary, where to divide the following words. Write out each word's syllables, with hyphens marking the division points.

   emissary   _____

   fortieth   _____

   sentimental   _____

   hygienist   _____

   precarious   _____

Recap

1. Parentheses can enclose explanation or details

   The bat (a symbolic animal for the Incas) flew away.

2. Parentheses should enclose publisher information in a footnote.

   Malcolm Donald, *The Energy Crisis* (New York: Benson Press, 1976), p. 274.

3. Dashes may separate a series from the rest of the sentence.

   The early Romantic poets—Blake, Wordsworth, Coleridge—shared an interest in human emotion.

4. Dashes may mark off an afterthought.

   The group finally elected Harrison—who, by the way, voted for his opponent.

   Dashes may separate a parenthetical comment.

   Smooth, rounded rocks—the kind found in stream beds—provide attractive ground cover for garden areas and entries.

5. Hyphens mark divisions within hyphenated compound words.

   father-in-law

   All compound numbers from twenty-one to ninety-nine are hyphenated.

6. Hyphens appear to divide words into syllables when division is necessary at a line-end.

   bi-o-de-grad-a-ble

Posttest: Parentheses, Dashes, and Hyphens

Insert appropriate parentheses in the first five sentences.

1. Benny spent half of the reward on a supercharger a device to increase carburetor capacity.
2. The viola cousin to the violin produces a deeper tone.
3. The English love shepherd's pie a mixture of vegetables, beef, and potatoes.
4. Uncle Ralph dusted off his grandfather's blunderbuss an old gun with a flaring muzzle.
5. The tortilla a flat Mexican cake made of flour or corn meal can be cut, fried, and salted to make tasty chips.

Insert appropriate dashes in the next five sentences.

6. Mervin's Pond not at all the peaceful setting I had anticipated turned out to be an industrial waste site.

7. The private saluted the sergeant an act motivated more by fear than by respect.
8. We eventually found an oak hall-tree with the original brass hooks still intact a rarity, especially in the case of pre-1890 pieces.
9. The colorful caravan camels, goats, children, chickens paused just long enough to strip the trees of pomegranates.
10. Spread out across her desk were the tools of writing paper, pencils, pens, erasers, scissors, tape, and a typewriter.

Insert appropriate hyphens in the next four sentences, and in the last item divide the word with hyphens.

11. An old man of war sailed into the harbor on the twenty sixth day of May.
12. The physicist explained steady state theory to the one hundred forty two students in the lecture hall.
13. His mother in law declared that she would buy only a car with a water cooled engine.
14. One half of the students did not know the names of their own great grandfathers.
15. Rewrite the word *ambiguous,* placing hyphens between the

    syllables: _____

Assignment

Edit the following paragraph by adding parentheses, dashes, and hyphens where they are appropriate. If you find any incorrect uses of them, make corrections. Use a dictionary whenever necessary. Remember that in some cases your decision is a matter of judgment, since more than one possibility may be acceptable.

Asteroids small planets with diameters from a fraction of a mile to nearly five-hundred miles may someday provide us with an almost limitless source of minerals. Scientists believe that many asteroids contain large amounts of several of the metals most important to earth's industries iron, nickel, copper, and cobalt. Using minerals from outer-space is not an entirely new idea. In ancient times as well as during recorded history, meteorites chunks of asteroid-like rock and metal that occasionally fall to earth have been a source of iron and other metals. In the future, astronauts may use space-ships to evaluate the mineral content of asteroids that pass near the earth. A small asteroid perhaps five-football-fields across might contain four-hundred-million tons of pure nickel and iron. At the 1982 price of about $3.50 a pound, the market-value of the refined nickel alone would be $120 billion. The value of the iron would be similar, and the worth of all the minerals in such an asteroid might be more than $300 billion a very respectable sum! Profits (from asteroid-mining) would depend, of course, on the cost of bringing the asteroid into a near-earth orbit not a small problem, nor a cheap one. However, the enormous value of the minerals not to speak of their growing scarcity on earth might encourage the development of new, relatively-cheap means of propulsion. Then these small planetoids could be brought close to the earth where their ores could be conveniently extracted.

Chapter 16
Capitalization

Two general conventions apply to capitalization in English. First, capital letters signal beginnings, for example, the beginning of a sentence, or sometimes the beginning of a direct quotation.

After six o'clock, we left.

Hearing a noise, she called, "Who's there?"

Second, capital letters identify proper nouns (France, Shakespeare) and the adjectives derived from them (French, Shakespearian). Proper nouns are names of specific persons, places, and things.

Thomas Jefferson   Milwaukee   Columbia River

Yellowstone National Park   Acme Food Company

After the Pretest, we will give you practice with some of the most important conventions of capitalization.

Pretest: Capitalization

In the sentences below, circle the letters that require capitalization.

1. many readers love *alice's adventures in wonderland* and *through the looking glass,* by lewis carroll.
2. much less known than those two favorites, however, is another work by carroll, *the hunting of the snark.* one wonders what the snark is. although the author never tells us exactly, one poetic line of his reads "for the snark was a boojum, you see."

3. lewis carroll was the pen name of the shy oxford don charles dodgson, who lived in victorian england.
4. during the nineteenth century his works were at first taken to be primarily for children, with their nonsensical wit and strange characters like humpty dumpty, the jabberwock, and the cheshire cat.
5. in england and the united states today, the wonderland books are both enjoyed by readers of all ages and seriously studied by scholars of literature and psychology.

16a   First Words of Sentences and Direct Quotations

The beginnings of sentences and direct quotations are marked by capital letters, as we have already seen. In addition, lines of poetry usually begin with a capital letter, as in the case of this short poem called "New Year's Dawn."

Sunrise over smooth curve
Of cheek and brow,
Golden aura glows
After cool blue starlight.

16b   Proper Nouns and Adjectives

The convention that proper nouns and the adjectives derived from them be capitalized applies to a variety of words and phrases.

Names and initials of persons and whatever titles precede a name

Alex Haley   Uncle Bill   General MacArthur   Professor Smith
BUT: my uncle   a general   that professor

Names and initials of specific places and major geographic areas

Catalina Island   Lake Michigan   Detroit   the South
BUT: an island   a lake   to drive south

Names of organizations and their members; names of ships, planes, and spacecraft

Smithsonian Institution   Roman Catholic Church   Catholics
the *Sea Princess*   Lindbergh's *Spirit of St. Louis*   the space shuttle
Columbia

Names of ethnic groups, races, nationalities, and languages

Chicano   Caucasian   Hungarian   French

Names of historical periods and events, days, months, and holidays

the Renaissance   World War II   Tuesday   July   Thanksgiving

16c Titles of Literary and Artistic Works

In the titles of books, plays, poems, musical compositions, films, and other works of art and literature, the first word and all other words (with a few exceptions) are capitalized. The exceptions include articles (*a, an, the*), prepositions (*in, on, with,* and the like), and conjunctions of fewer than five letters (*and, or, but,* and so on); these words are not capitalized.

Richard Wright's *Native Son* (book)   Thomas Mann's "Death in Venice" (story)

Oscar Wilde's "The Importance of Being Earnest" (play)   Berlioz's *Harold in Italy* (symphony)

Rodin's *Burghers of Calais* (sculpture)   Vermeer's *Head of a Young Girl* (painting)

Star Wars (film)   *Swan Lake* (ballet)

Exercise 16.1 | In the sentences below, circle the letters that require capitalization.

1. the dance entertainer, the hoofer, has been with us since colonial days.
2. from early "cloggers" and tap dancers to today's thirty-six radio city music hall rockettes, dancing has never ceased to be one of america's most popular branches of show business.
3. classical ballet was imported to the new world from europe.
4. george washington himself admired the artistry of john durang, son of a soldier of the american revolution, and the first profes-

sional dancer of note to be produced by the new united states of america.

5. early in this century a new form of theater dance evolved in the united states that rejected the rigidities of ballet technique, as well as its fanciful, fairy tale themes.

6. called modern dance for want of a better name, this new style was pioneered by innovators like isadora duncan (1878–1927), ruth st. denis (1878–1968) and ted shawn (1891–1972).

7. today, dance groups like the repertory dance theatre of utah are attempting to recreate classics of the recent past before all direct knowledge of the early days of modern dance is lost.

8. at its home on the campus of the university of utah at salt lake city, the repertory dance theatre works at restaging works like ruth st. denis's *the incense* and charles weidman's *the moth and the star.*

9. a great deal of research in utah and on both the west coast and the east coast is being dedicated to rediscovering the pre-world war II roots of modern dance.

10. in sharp contrast to an earlier generation for whom "dance" meant arthur murray and a ballroom, children and adults today are studying modern and classical dance in studios all across america.

Recap

1. Capitalize the first word of sentences, direct quotations, and most lines of poetry.

   She looked at me and said, "Well?"

   Education forms the common mind,
   As the twig is bent, so the tree's inclined.

2. Capitalize the names and initials of persons, places, and geographical areas.

   Sanford P. Ramsey   the Old West   New York

3. Capitalize the names of organizations and their members.

   Rotary Club   Rotarians

4. Capitalize the names of ships, planes, and spacecraft.

   the *Queen Elizabeth*   the *Enterprise*

5. Capitalize the names of ethnic groups, races, nationalities, and languages.

   Jewish   Lithuanian   Native American

6. Capitalize the names of days, months, holidays, and historical periods and events.

   Friday   September   the Depression   Labor Day

7. Capitalize the first word and all the other major words in titles of books, plays, poems, and musical compositions, films, and works of art.

   War and Peace   Afternoon of a Faun

   "Nobody Knows the Trouble I've Seen"

Posttest: Capitalization

In the sentences below, circle the letters that require capitalization.

1. from june to november, tropical depressions frequently form over the atlantic just above the equator.
2. the national weather service, at its hurricane center in miami, florida, monitors each tropical depression.
3. approximately one out of five tropical depressions intensifies into a full-fledged hurricane that may threaten life and property in the caribbean basin and along the east coast.
4. the first person to understand that hurricanes are giant circular weather patterns was william c. redfield of middletown, connecticut, an amateur meteorologist.
5. by comparing such data as the patterns of fallen trees and reports of ships' captains, redfield reached the conclusion that a hurricane was a massive whirlwind. he published his discovery in the *american journal of science* in 1831.
6. lovers of jazz immediately recognize such classics as benny goodman playing "body and soul" or billie holiday singing "all of me."

7. my friend ron was surprised by how much he liked the poem "tyger, tyger, burning bright" in william blake's book *songs of innocence and of experience.*

8. a polish cosmonaut joined two russians in a rocket flight to the soviet space station.

9. the san francisco end of the golden gate bridge arches over historic civil war-era fort winfield scott (now known as fort point).

10. professor andrews required each student to buy the *practical english handbook* by watkins and dillingham.

Assignment

Proofread the following paragraph, correcting mistakes in capitalization.

one contemporary school of architecture claims that the form of a building must follow its function. perhaps this simply means that the form "stands for" the function of the building. the form of trinity church, on broadway at wall street in new york city, resembles that of chartres cathedral in france; we recognize their similar functions by their similar forms. the form of the union carbide building, a tall rectangular skyscraper in new york city, tells us it houses offices. but clearly the edict that form follows function must mean more than that form stands for function. one of frank lloyd wright's last and most famous works—the solomon r. guggenheim museum, a graceful structure of curving lines—contrasts sharply, perhaps too sharply, with the box-like high-rise buildings that surround it. we are not surprised to learn that the building was originally planned for a location in central park. evidently the form of a building ought to take into account the way the building functions in its environment, not just in isolation.

APPENDICES

Appendix A
Spelling

"I just can't spell" describes an attitude, not a reality. The truth is that every student can spell correctly by following one rule: *use the dictionary*. This simple advice assumes, of course, that the student knows *when* to use the dictionary to check a doubtful spelling. Some internal editor must select which words to check. In a 500-word essay, for example, it would be impractical to check each and every word.

You can strengthen your internal editing abilities in four ways:

Look up any word about which you have even the slightest doubt. Professional writers and editors reach for their dictionaries often.

Double-check your writing for properly spelled word endings (*-able, -ible, -tion, -sion, -s/-es, -ed,* and *-y/-ey*).

Double-check your writing for common reversals and substitutions (*ei* for *ie, f* for *ph, y* for *i, ai* for *ia, s* for *c, k* for *c, ous* for *ious, ence* for *ance, z* for *s,* and *ue* for *eu*).

Watch especially for the following *College Spelling Demons:*

absence	arguing	choose
accidentally	argument	chose
accommodate	arithmetic	committee
accumulate	athletic	conscience
advice	attendance	conscious
advise	beginning	definitely
a lot	beneficial	desperate
allot	benefited	dictionary
amateur	break	disappearance
analyze	Britain	disastrous
appearance	bureau	dissatisfied
arctic	business	effect

eligible	miracle	referred
embarrass	mysterious	restaurant
eminent	necessary	rhythm
environment	neurotic	sacrilegious
equipped	neutral	schedule
especially	ninety	seize
exaggerate	notable	separate
excellence	noticeable	sergeant
existence	occurred	severely
experience	occurrence	sieve
familiar	omitted	similar
February	optimistic	sophomore
foreign	parallel	stationary
forty	paralyze	stationery
fourth	pastime	studying
generally	performance	subtle
government	personal	successful
grammar	personnel	surprise
height	physical	tendency
heiress	possession	than
homemade	precede	then
humorous	preferred	their, there, they're
hygiene	prejudice	thorough
immediately	principal	through
incredible	principle	to, too, two
independence	privilege	tragedy
interesting	probably	tries
irresistible	proceed	trouble
its, it's	professor	truly
laid	pronunciation	typically
led	prophecy	usually
lead	prophesy	unbelievable
lightning	qualm	utterance
loneliness	quarrel	vaccinate
loose	quiet	vain
lose	quite	vein
losing	quizzes	villain
marriage	receive	weather
mathematics	receiving	weird
maybe	referee	wholly
miniature	reference	writing

Appendix B
The Growth of the Essay

In the following step-by-step example, we can observe the development of a five-paragraph essay from idea to polished draft. We shall follow the "Essay Blueprint" guidelines described on pages 136–137.

Step 1

We prepare mentally. We've cleared the decks of other competing interests and activities. We're not afraid to write; in fact, we're looking forward to the task. We have allowed plenty of time before the essay must be handed in.

We have decided to write about graffiti. Though we are not experts on the subject, we do have attitudes, observations, and memories. We *know ourselves* and feel no obligation to sound like an encyclopedia or a prophet. We choose to write in a natural, straightforward way.

We *know our audience*, in this case our composition instructor and the members of an English class. They will appreciate interesting observations expressed in a vivid manner. They will yawn with boredom if we wander from the topic or belabor the obvious. We want to interest and stimulate them.

We can get to *know our topic* by jotting down responses to the twelve questions for brainstorming.

1. If (no one) (everyone) had
   _____ graffiti _____ , how would
   the world be different?

—more beautiful neighborhoods

—less angry residents

_____

_____

_____

2. What kind of people find
    _____graffiti_____ especially
    tempting, interesting, or valu-
    able? Why?

    —frustrated people trying to
    make a mark
    —people who want to set
    boundaries on a territory
    _____
    _____

3. For certain periods of my life, I
    was almost unaware (or partic-
    ularly aware) of ____graffiti____ .
    Why?

    —I didn't know what the
    scrawls meant
    —there wasn't much graffiti
    where I lived
    _____
    _____

4. _____Graffiti_____ is/are usually
    associated with a certain part of
    the world. Why?

    —usually associated with
    ghettoes
    —gangs are more common
    there
    _____
    _____

5. Few (many) people lie awake at
    night thinking about ___graffiti___ .
    Why?

    —they fear violence
    —they are afraid to paint over
    the graffiti
    _____
    _____
    _____

6. _____Graffiti_____ can have an impact upon emotions. How?

—to the gang, a mark of accomplishment

—for residents, an insult and challenge

7. _____Graffiti_____, in spite of its surface simplicity, has/have a deeper significance. What?

—marks territory

—expresses identity

—way of hurting others

—challenges rival gangs

8. _____Graffiti_____ arouse(s) widely different memories. What are they?

—swastikas of the Nazis

—excitement and fear of gang neighborhood

9. _____Graffiti_____ can be divided into major parts. What are they?

—child graffiti: "Billy X"

—loner graffiti: "Remember John Lennon"

—gang graffiti: "White Shoes Rule"

10. _____Graffiti_____ might be
wholly unnecessary if . . .

—gangs cared about all residents in their territories

—anger between gangs could be lessened

11. _____Graffiti_____ is not the way it was in the past. Why?

—used to be unthinkable

—social groups all opposed it

12. When I think of _____graffiti_____ , three images come to mind. Why? What are they?

—scrawl on a wall

—a resident shaking his or her head in dismay

—a kid with a spray can at 2 a.m.

Step 2

We *plan the architecture* of the essay. We can circle the most promising ideas among our jottings above. Then we will use *limiting circles* to discover how our specific or limited topic relates to the general idea of graffiti.

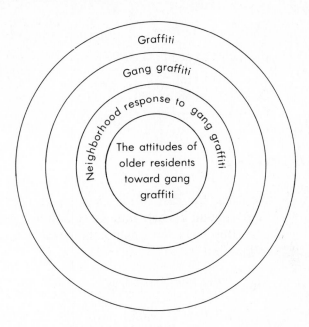

With the help of limiting circles, we see the target toward which the essay will aim: the attitudes of elderly residents toward gang graffiti.

Step 3

We *restate our limited essay topic as a problem.*

Limited Topic	Problem
attitudes of the elderly	Elderly residents feel terror
toward gang graffiti	over gang graffiti

Step 4

We *choose or invent a suitable pattern* for the development of our thoughts. In this case, the Personal essay pattern (number 2) seems to fit well.

The Personal Essay
A.   Once I felt . . .
B.   Something happened
C.   Now I feel . . .
D.   Now I can or will . . .
E.   Looking back, I see . . .

Step 5

We *follow the cues of our chosen essay pattern.* First, we write down the basic content of each paragraph, noting details we may want to use. These first efforts will serve as building blocks for the actual paragraphs of our rough draft.

Pattern: the Personal Essay   *Details*

A.   I used to feel graffiti was harmless.   —the graffiti on Hudson St.

B.   Mrs. Donnelly died from fright after the gang sprayed her house.   —Mrs. Donnelly in the hospital
—the words "BURN KILL BURN" on her white cottage

C.   I think about the terror that elderly residents must feel in gang neighborhoods.   —Mr. Brolston's efforts to repaint his drug store
—the gang's revenge

D.   I can support a legislative effort to fight graffiti.   —bill provides for strict laws and teams trained to work with gangs

E. I was part of the problem. I   —None of Mr. Brolston's neigh-
    believed graffiti was harmless,   bors cared enough to help
    and I ignored the terror of   him when his drug store was
    others.   sprayed.

We now have a working outline for our essay. We know approximately what we want to say. We have selected vivid, specific details and examples.

Step 6

We *write.* Our preparation pays off as we follow our working outline, letting ourselves write in a natural, free way. There will be time later to edit, revise, and correct. Now we simply have to "let it out."

As we write, we remember the importance of paragraph development. We know several patterns for paragraph organization—for example, Topic Sentence/Expansion/Illustration/"So What?" Conclusion—and, when we wish, we can fashion patterns of our own.

Rough Draft

(Note: Even though our rough draft appears in typeset form, you may wish to write your rough drafts first in pen or pencil. Later on, you will want to type the final version.)

(A.)   There was a time when I used to think that graffiti was just a harmless prank. As I saw it, scrawls on walls and doors seemed to be no more serious than the marks our ancestors carved in tree bark: "John loveth Mary." In fact, as a ten-year-old I got a charge out of watching the groovy graffiti flash by along Hudson St. when I took the bus across town to visit my grandfather. Graffiti, like tin cans tied to the bride and groom's car, just seemed to be part of the unsightly, harmless, and mildly amusing clutter of the city.

(B.)   My mind was changed abruptly when my grandfather, in tears, called to tell us that his next door neighbor, a woman in her eighties named Mrs. Donnelly, had just died from a heart attack. Four days before, he told us, someone had sprayed some graffiti across the face of her house. My grandfather had offered to help scrub off the orange paint. However, she was afraid and insisted that he leave the paint alone. Two days later she died in the hospital, still afraid.

(C.)   Since that day I've had a different view of it. It may be true that teen-agers are expressing their identities and social needs through graffiti—but I think first of Mrs. Donnelly. Whether they mean to or not, gangs are terrifying neighborhood residents, particularly the elderly. When old Mr. Brolston's drug store on Hudson St. got sprayed, he repainted the store. The next night his windows were smashed. The store was resprayed in angry red scrawls. Now Mr. Brolston says he won't repaint. He says he will close the store. On his walls now, as on others up and down the street, the graffiti grows old—a silent and chilling way of telling how long the neighborhood has been afraid.

(D.)   Although I can't physically stop the gangs from defacing the houses of my grandfather and his neighbors, I can act against such senseless cruelty. I'm supporting a bill in the State legislature making parents financially responsible for the damaging graffiti of their children. The bill provides funds for stricter law enforcement and for teams trained to work with gangs in cleaning up neighborhoods. When the bill becomes law, people like my grandfather and Mr. Brolston can take a stand against the defacement of their property. Who will back them up? They will have the support of strong laws and effective social programs.

(E.)   When I think back to my naive view of gang graffiti as harmless mischief, I realize that I was an unwitting part of the problem. I accepted it, and didn't care. My grandfather told me that, in his day, no one would have even thought of spraying obscene words on someone else's property. All of society—neighbors, fellow workers, even friends—would rise up against the culprit. But in our day, none of Mr. Brolston's neighbors cared enough to help him watch over his store. No one called the police the night the windows were smashed. Whether the neighbors were too afraid to act or, like me, too naive to act, the result was the same: a long-time elderly resident was terrified, and the gang ruled. I now understand that in ignoring the gang graffiti around me, I ignored the terror of innocent people.

Step 7

We can now *polish the rough draft.* We use each of the fifteen points of style as a magnifying glass to examine and repair portions of the rough draft. We check spelling, punctuation and grammar with care.

Notice in the following revision that numbered matters of style appear in the margin to explain the changes in the rough draft. These notes are for your information, and need not appear in your own revisions unless your instructor wishes them there.

The Revised Draft

Margin annotations:

(5) *Eliminating wordiness*
(3) *Emphasizing important words through placement*
(9) *Avoiding trite and slang expressions*

(1) *Using active voice*

(4) *Being specific*

(3) *Emphasizing important words through placement*
(4) *Being specific*
(4) *Being specific*
(5) *Eliminating wordiness*

(1) *Using active voice*
(1) *Using active voice*

(14) *Choosing words carefully*

~~There was a time when~~ I used to think that graffiti was just a harmless prank. ~~As I saw it,~~ Scrawls on walls and doors seemed to be no more serious than the marks our ancestors carved in tree bark: "John loveth Mary." In fact, as a ten-year-old I ~~got a charge out of~~ *liked* watching the ~~groovy~~ *strange* graffiti flash by along Hudson St. when I took the bus across town to visit my grandfather. Graffiti, like tin cans tied to the bride and groom's car, just seemed to be part of the unsightly, harmless, and mildly amusing clutter of the city.

I changed my mind ~~My mind was changed~~ abruptly when my grandfather, in tears, called to tell us that his next door neighbor, a woman in her eighties named Mrs. Donnelly, had just died from a heart attack. Four days before, he told us, ~~someone~~ *the neighborhood gang* had sprayed ~~some graffiti~~ *"BURN KILL BURN"* across the face of her ~~house~~ *white cottage*. My grandfather had offered to help scrub off the orange paint. *Near hysteria, she* ~~However, she was afraid and~~ insisted that he leave the paint alone. Two days later she died in the hospital, ~~still afraid~~ *mumbling "they'll burn my house."*

Since that day I've had a different view of ~~it. It may be true that~~ *graffiti. Some* teen-agers ~~are~~ express~~ing~~ their identities and social needs through graffiti—but I think first of Mrs. Donnelly. Whether they mean to or not, gangs are terrifying neighborhood residents, particularly the elderly. When old Mr. Brolston's drug store on Hudson St. ~~got sprayed~~ *the gang sprayed*, he repainted the store immediately. The next night ~~his windows were smashed.~~ *the gang smashed his windows.* The store was resprayed in angry red scrawls. Now Mr. Brolston says he won't repaint. He says he will close the store. On his walls now, as on others up and down the street, the graffiti grows old—a silent and chilling ~~way of telling~~ *calendar measuring* how long the neighborhood has been afraid.

Although I can't physically stop the gangs from defacing the houses of my grandfather and his neighbors, I can act against such senseless cruelty. I'm supporting a bill in the State legislature making parents financially responsible for the damaging graffiti of their children. The bill provides funds for stricter law enforcement and for teams trained to work with gangs in cleaning up neighborhoods. When the bill becomes law, people like my grandfather and Mr. Brolston can take a stand against

(13) *Avoiding unnecessary questions*

the defacement of their property. ~~Who will back them up?~~ They will have the support of strong laws and effective social programs.

When I think back on my naive view of gang graffiti as harmless mischief, I realize that I was an unwitting part of the problem. I accepted

(4) *Being specific*

graffiti,
~~it,~~ and didn't care. My grandfather told me that⊙ in his day⊙ no one would have ~~even~~ thought of spraying obscene words on someone else's property. All of society—neighbors, fellow workers, even friends—would rise up against the culprit. But in our day, none of Mr. Brolston's neighbors cared enough to help him watch over his store. No one called the police the

(1) *Using active voice*

the gang smashed the windows.
night ~~the windows were smashed.~~ Whether the neighbors were too afraid

(1) *Using active voice*

a tragedy occurred: the gang terrified
to act or, like me, too naive, ~~the result was the same: a long time, elderly~~
an elderly resident.
~~resident was terrified, and the gang ruled.~~ I now understand that in ignoring the gang graffiti around me, I ignored the terror of innocent people.

Step 8

At last, we are ready to type the final draft of our essay. We've worked hard to say what we wanted to say. We've eliminated many errors. With so much effort involved in the essay, we look forward to finding out how others respond to our writing. What do they like? What do they dislike? What do they misunderstand? Constructive criticism can help us refine our writing skills.

The Polished Draft

Graffiti Can Spell Terror for the Elderly

I used to think that graffiti was just a harmless prank. Scrawls on walls and doors seemed to be no more serious than the marks our ancestors carved in tree bark: "John loveth Mary." In fact, as a ten-year-old, I liked watching the strange graffiti flash by along Hudson St. when I took the bus across town to visit my grandfather. Graffiti, like tin cans tied to the bride and groom's car, just seemed to be part of the unsightly, harmless, and mildly amusing clutter of the city.

I changed my mind abruptly when my grandfather, in tears, called to tell us that his next door neighbor, a woman in her eighties named Mrs. Donnelly, had just died from a heart attack. Four days before, he told us, the neighborhood gang had sprayed "BURN KILL BURN" across the face of her white cottage. My grandfather had offered to help scrub off the orange paint. Near hysteria, she insisted that he leave the paint alone. Two days later she died in the hospital, mumbling "they'll burn my house."

Since that day I've had a different view of graffiti. Some teen-agers express their identities and social needs through graffiti—but I think first of Mrs. Donnelly. Whether they mean to or not, gangs are terrifying neighborhood residents, particularly the elderly. When the gang sprayed old Mr. Brolston's drug store on Hudson St., he repainted the store immediately. The next night the gang smashed his windows. The store was resprayed in angry red scrawls. Now Mr. Brolston won't repaint. He says he will close the store. On his walls now, as on others up and down the street, the graffiti grows old—a silent and chilling calendar measuring how long the neighborhood has been afraid.

Although I can't physically stop the gangs from defacing the houses of my grandfather and his neighbors, I can act against such senseless cruelty. I'm supporting a bill in the State legislature making parents financially responsible for the damaging graffiti of their children. The bill provides funds for stricter law enforcement and for teams trained to work with gangs in cleaning up neighborhoods. When the bill becomes law, people like my grandfather and Mr. Brolston can take a stand against the defacement of their property. They will have the support of strong laws and effective social programs.

When I think back on my naive view of gang graffiti as harmless mischief, I realize that I was an unwitting part of the problem. I accepted graffiti, and didn't care. My grandfather told me that in his day no one would have thought of spraying obscene words on someone else's property. All of society—neighbors, fellow workers, even friends—would rise up against the culprit. But in our day, none of Mr. Brolston's neighbors cared enough to help him watch over his store. No one called the police the night the gang smashed the windows. Whether the neighbors were too afraid to act or, like me, too naive, a tragedy occurred: the gang terrified an elderly resident. I now understand that in ignoring the gang graffiti around me, I ignored the terror of innocent people.

Appendix C

A Short Guide to the Long Paper

After a dormant period in the 1970s, the term paper is making a comeback at many colleges and universities. The odds are high that more than once during your college education you will face the challenge of the extended essay, which is variously called a research, library, or term paper. Often the paper will count heavily in your instructor's evaluation of your success in the course.

What follows is a step-by-step recipe of sorts for the term paper. Note that this pattern is not the only pattern. Your instructor may have a different model in mind. You will do well to check before beginning work.

Step 1   Decide

With your instructor's help, *settle on a topic* relevant to the course. *Limit your topic*, using the technique of limiting circles presented in Section 6b and illustrated in Appendix B. Then, *convert your topic to a concern*. Again, Chapter 6 (Section 6b) can guide you in this matter. *Discuss your final limited concern* with your instructor.

Step 2   Read

Devote time and energy to general reading about your area of concern. At this point, you may choose not to take elaborate notes. Often it is helpful to get the "lay of the land" regarding your subject. Browse through library materials that may serve your needs. Consult your librarian about the different catalogues and indexes that might help you find articles and books about your subject.

Step 3   Outline

Use an essay blueprint sheet from Chapter 6 to map out a rough working outline. Don't become discouraged at this point. The act of conceptualizing what needs to be said and where to say it is a difficult intellectual activity. Be "tough-minded," in William James's phrase, forcing yourself to think clearly without excuse or compromise. At the same time, be patient with yourself without becoming lax. You are not committed to the items on this rough working outline. It provides merely a starting point, always subject to revision and improvement.

Step 4   Research

With your rough outline in hand, begin to seek hard evidence and expert opinion through library research. Consider all of the following sources:

Your instructor may recommend particularly valuable books or articles.

Your librarian may lead you directly to pertinent library resources on your topic.

The card catalogue will list, by title, author, and often subject, the individual works dealing with your area of interest.

Consult the periodical indexes. Each month *The Readers' Guide to Periodical Literature* gathers together article titles from hundreds of magazines. Other indexes appear in journals devoted to a particular subject. If, for example, you are looking for information on the poetry of Keats, you would do well to see the annual bibliography of Keats studies gathered together by the Keats-Shelley Association in the *Keats-Shelley Journal*. Since there are hundreds of specialized journals and bibliographies, your best guide will be your librarian.

A relatively new research tool at many libraries is the computer search. By providing your librarian with key words from your area of interest (such as *Medical Insurance*), you can have a computer search an HEW-compiled file of thousands of books, articles, dissertations, and even pamphlets. Sometimes within a day you'll receive back a read-out of titles likely to serve your needs. The actual articles can be found in microfiche-card files and then read, sometimes even photo-copied, with a microfiche reader.

What To Do When You Find What You're Looking For

Let us say that for a biology term paper you are trying to prove that small birds lay fewer eggs than big birds. In your research, you come across a book on hummingbirds by I. Kant Swallow. Dr. Swallow, as an expert, writes that " . . . most species of hummingbirds common to North and South America lay only one or two eggs per nesting season." You know that this bit of information, together with other data, will help to make your point in a solid way. First, *make a bibliography* card containing the following information:

Author's name, full title, city of publication, publisher, and date of publication.

Swallow, I. Kant. *Hummingbirds of the Americas.*
New York: Jebson Press, 1980

Now you are free to write as many *research note cards* as necessary based on information from Swallow's book.

Notice that the *research note card* need only contain Swallow's name, not complete book information. On your note card, write the evidence or quotation you want to use. You may also want to write brief notes to yourself.

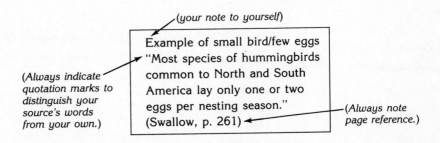

(your note to yourself)

Example of small bird/few eggs
"Most species of hummingbirds common to North and South America lay only one or two eggs per nesting season."
(Swallow, p. 261)

(Always indicate quotation marks to distinguish your source's words from your own.)

(Always note page reference.)

After a period of such research, you will have gathered many bibliographical and research note cards. Sort them so they correspond in a general way to the major sections of your paper (as organized on the essay blueprint sheet). Now the actual writing begins.

Step 5   Write

Following the method practiced in Chapter 6 and further illustrated in Appendix B, write the first draft of your paper. In drawing your research note cards into your writing, *avoid the four fatal pitfalls:*

> *Plagiarism.* Don't use others' words as your own. If their exact words are valuable to your argument, first *explain* their importance in your own words and then *quote* your source with full credit.
>
> *Stringing together note cards.* Some writers make the mistake of connecting note card to note card with only a few words of their own analysis and argument. Try to weave your research quotations smoothly into fully developed paragraphs filled primarily with your own thinking.

> Small birds typically lay fewer eggs. The hummingbird, as I. Kant Swallow points out, "lays only one or two eggs per nesting season."[6] The canary, similarly, . . .

Notice that the writer did not use the whole quotation. Only the pertinent words were used, and they mesh smoothly with the course of the on-going argument. The number at the end of the quotation, as explained in Step 7, refers to a footnote containing information on your source.

> *Unannounced sources.* Don't drop evidence or quotations on your reader without appropriate introduction.

NOT: Small birds lay few eggs. "Most species of hummingbirds common to North and South America lay only one or two eggs per nesting season."[6] The canary similarly, . . .

INSTEAD: Small birds lay few eggs. The hummingbird, as I. Kant Swallow points out, "lays only one or two eggs per nesting season."[6] The canary similarly, . . .

> *Underkill and overkill.* Exercise judgment in how many quotations of evidence and expert opinion are necessary to make your point. For instance, for the point about small birds laying few eggs, probably three or four examples of small birds, along with an expert generalization, would suffice. Too few citations make the reader dubious; too many quotations make the reader impatient.

Step 6   Revise and Rewrite

Use all of the suggestions found in Section 6d. By techniques explained and practiced there, refine the logical and stylistic development of your paper.

Step 7   Footnote

Number each citation of evidence or expert opinion, including paraphrased passages, throughout your paper. Footnote numbers are usually placed slightly above the line at the end of the citation. Either at the bottom of each page or at the end of the paper, list the sources for each quotation by using the number appearing in the text.

Some disciplines, particularly scientific fields, require a different footnote style from that given here. Check with your instructor if you are unsure which style to use. Once a style has been chosen, however, the form for footnotes is fixed and specific. Here is a common footnote style for general college writing.

The First Time You Refer to a Source

1. Books by a single author

   John O. White, *Sailing* (Boston: Thomas Bros. Publishers, 1980), p. 92.

2. Books with two authors

   Joseph Prince and Joy Traler, *Once in Time* (New York: Krisler Press, 1964), p. 195.

3. Books with three or more authors

   Sharon Anderson and others, *What's Wrong with Joe?* (St. Louis: Donnell Press, 1980), p. 27.

4. An edited book

   a collection

   Frank Dennison, ed., *The Cowboy in New Mexico* (Los Angeles: Spur Press, 1974), p. 94.

author's works

Henry David Thoreau, *Collected Poems,* ed. Carl Bode (Chicago: Packard and Co., 1943), p. 145.

a translation

Arthur Schlegel, *Romantic Theory,* trans. S. M. Hurona (Berlin: Schmelzer Press, 1961), p. 45.

an encyclopedia

"Bananas," Encyclopaedia Britannica, 1976, 14, p. 941.

5. A newspaper

"Even the I.R.S. Doesn't Know," *Arizona Republic,* May 4, 1952, Section B, p. 14. (Author appears first if known)

6. A magazine

"The Selling of Cells," *Time,* Jan. 21, 1972, p. 36. (Author appears first if known)

7. A journal

Carol Bannister, "Computer Anxiety," *Studies in Computer Learning,* 16, No. 3 (1982), 31-39.

Later References to the Same Source

It is simple: refer to the author's last name, then the page.

White, p. 95.

If the author is not known, refer simply to the title and page.

"The Selling of Cells," p. 38.

Step 8   Add a Bibliography

In alphabetical order by last name (or title, if the author is unknown), list those sources you used in preparing the paper.

BOOK: Abramson, R. L. *Night Thoughts.* Chicago: Zeus, 1969.

MAGAZINE: "Better Carrots Through Hydroponics," *Agri-World,* 179 (September 1, 1974), 25.

NEWSPAPERS: "Poisonous Carrots Kill Family," Los Angeles *Times*, August 10, 1975, p. 4.

ENCYCLOPEDIA: Weisfeld, W. P. "Antidotes." *Encyclopedia Americana,* 1, 49.

Step 9   Add a Title Page

While your instructor may have special title page requirements, it is customary to center the following information in the top half of the typed page:

TRADITIONAL THEMES IN NAVAJO WEAVING
by
Charles Toyon

American Studies 365
January 22, 1983

for
Professor Carla Laughton

Step 10   Assemble the Paper

From top to bottom:

Title page

Text pages

Footnote page(s), if footnotes have not been typed at the bottom of each page

Bibliography page(s)

Usually you should make a photocopy of your paper before submitting it. While the legend of the absent-minded professor is well-known, its companion—the trash-happy janitor—is learned the hard way each semester.

Index